GET THE GUY

GET THE GUY

HOW TO BE THE KIND OF WOMAN
THE KIND OF MAN YOU WANT TO MARRY
WOULD WANT TO MARRY

DOUGLAS WILSON

CANON  PRESS

MOSCOW, IDAHO

Published by Canon Press

P. O. Box 8729, Moscow, Idaho 83843

800-488-2034 | www.canonpress.com

Douglas Wilson, *Get the Guy: How to Be the Kind of Woman the Kind of Man You Want to Marry Would Want to Marry*

Library of Congress Cataloging-in-Publication Data

Wilson, Douglas, 1953- author.

Get the guy : how to be the kind of woman the kind of man you want to marry would want to marry / Douglas Wilson.

Moscow, Idaho : Canon Press, 2023.

 Provided by publisher.

LCCN 2022049597 | ISBN 9781957905389 (paperback)

LCSH: Dating (Social customs) | Single women—Religious life. | Christian women—Religious life.

Classification: LCC HQ800.2 .W53 2023 | DDC 306.73—dc23/eng/20230110

LC record available at https://lccn.loc.gov/2022049597

23 24 25 26 27 28 29   10 9 8 7 6 5 4 3

To all my real nieces—Michalangela, Brook, Mallory,
Heather, Yeran, Sevan, Sarah, and Clara—who
didn't need the advice in this book any more than their
brothers did.

CONTENTS

ONE

AND AT LEAST SIX WITH CHUBBY CHEEKS

Dear Darla,

Thank you for writing—it was quite a pleasant surprise to hear from you. So your cousin Dawson told you about our correspondence, did he? And you thought it would be festive to get some corresponding advice for you and your girl friends? I mentioned your letter to Nancy, and she said something along the lines of, *"Why not?"* Although she might be looking over my shoulder a bit more with these letters . . .

Because I don't know your particular situation yet—I assume your next letter will fill me in—I think I would like to start by discussing the ecosystem your relationships are in. Or lack of relationships, as the case may be.

And so what do I mean by ecosystem? Relationships are like plants—they grow and flourish according to their own internal logic, meaning that a tulip grows as a tulip, a redwood as a redwood, an orchid as an orchid, and so on. Plants reproduce after their kind, which is the internal logic. But relationships (like plants) are also dependent upon external factors, like climate, soil, etc. Certain plants won't grow in certain places. Huckleberries don't grow at lower altitudes. Most lilacs don't grow down South. Orchids don't grow above the tree line.

Now if you and your friends are anything like the other young Christian women I know, your chief complaint has to do with the paucity of guys. Where are all the guys? Where did they all go? And then, when you are looking at the handful of guys who do hang around in your church community, you think to yourself, as the saying goes, "The odds may be good, but the goods are odd."

And once this complaint has settled in, the tendency is to blame the guys for not showing up. Where are they? It is a natural question, but I actually regard it as a very natural mistake.

Now please bear with me here—I am going to extend my analogy some. The relationship "plants" are not growing and flourishing, and these relationship plants take a girl half and a boy half. All the girls halves you know are willing and eager to be Christian wives and mothers, and so the blame falls naturally on the guys, who are clearly failing to get off the dime.

But perhaps the relationships aren't growing because the *climate* is not conducive to it. Oranges don't grow in the Yukon.

Now the guys are affected by the climate, just as the women are, but that climate is much larger than any particular set of individual choices. The kind of relationships that Christians want to see growing are relationships that grow readily when the surrounding culture is supportive. When that surrounding culture is *not* supportive, as ours most certainly is not, it is consequently difficult for relationships to form readily. And it is even more difficult for godly relationships to form. It is like wading up stream when the current is running hard the other way.

The individual aspect happens when John decides to ask Suzy out, or to call her father in the interest of getting to know her better. That is the individual action of a "relationship plant."

What are the factors that make up the climate? I am talking about parental expectations, career paths, vocational training, the movies we watch, the sermons we listen to, the way custody is apportioned in divorce cases, the ubiquity of pornography, the social expectation that marriages will normally occur in the late twenties instead of the early twenties, abortion culture, women in the work force, and the way everyone is on guard against the patriarchy.

Many of these elements are noticeably present within conservative evangelical churches, and even socially accepted. Say that a young woman in the church applies to and is accepted to the Naval Academy, and she is telling everyone that she wants to fly fighters off carriers. In the average evangelical church, who will be the odd man out? The woman who has this goal, or the person who tries to register some level of concern about it?

And even those aspects of the world's dominance here that cannot be openly embraced are issues where you see quiet acquiescence. Pornography will not be openly celebrated from the pulpit, but use of pornography within the congregation is nevertheless widespread. The more conservative churches would be the ones where you might find an accountability group or two trying to stem the tide.

So what I am saying is the fact that young people are postponing marriage, and the fact that we have numerous young women wishing that there were more guys around, and that the guys who are around would be more assertive and masculine, is in the first place a societal problem. It is not in the first instance a problem of John getting up the nerve to approach Suzy. That problem does enter into it, but it is a direct downstream consequence of what we have been telling John since he was two.

So the task of young Christian women is therefore two-fold. The first is the obvious individual one, one that applies to both men and women. Become the kind of person that the kind of person you would want to marry would want to marry. What does the Bible call women to do? Are you preparing for that?

The apostle Paul once warned a certain class of people not to "turn aside" after Satan. Just the sort of thing an apostle would tell Christians, right? Don't turn aside after Satan. Seems obvious: "For some are already turned aside after Satan" (1 Tim. 5:15).

But when this class of person was turning aside after Satan, what were they veering away *from*? What were they leaving behind? Well, the previous verse tells us: "I will therefore that the younger women marry, bear children, guide the house, give none occasion to the adversary to speak reproachfully" (1 Tim. 5:14).

Paul's instruction here is being given to the younger women—you and your girl friends. First, he wants them to marry, and you might be tempted to say that this is exactly what you want also. Isn't that why you wrote?

But Paul might be defining the vocation of marriage a little bit differently than twenty-first century Christian voices do. A woman today might want to find her BFF, marry him, and then go hiking with him across Europe to create memories. But marriage is a vocation, not a scrapbooking exercise.

And Paul says that women who turn aside after Satan are women who avoid marriage, avoid having babies, and who avoid the domestic arts. *That's* how women turn aside after Satan. And all God's people said *yikes*.

This is going to reveal certain things to you about the second way you can contribute to a solution. When confronted by what the Scriptures describe as the central domestic calling of women, notice your emotional reflex against that. Notice the objections (and the acknowledged exceptions) that crowd into your mind. Notice how you want to talk about Deborah all of a sudden. All of that is the climate talking. All of that is how you have been catechized by that climate. All of a sudden this mysterious climate thing I have been talking about has become very visible. All of a sudden it is palpable.

So do what you can to say and do things that conflict with the soft feminist *zeitgeist* that is pervasive in evangelical circles. Become a contrary voice in the climate. Do what you can to subvert the dominant paradigm. Do what you can to challenge the dominant paradigm.

Someone asks you, as they always do, what you want to do after you graduate. You should say

something like this: "I would like to have eight babies in a row. And I would like at least six of them to
have chubby *cheeks*!"

Your uncle,
Douglas

TWO

THE FRAUGHT TOPIC OF MODESTY

Dear Darla,

So here is a topic we should get out of the way early on. It has become, I am afraid, an inflammatory topic in our culture more broadly, and this despite being one that ought to be ranked as one of the most common sense issues ever. I bring this subject up, not because I have ever seen you having trouble with it, but because I know that it has to be an ongoing issue. Every time you shop for clothes it comes up as an issue, and it also comes up as a point of discussion with your friends.

I am talking about feminine modesty, and perhaps you have seen one of the periodic continent-wide sheets of flame that go up when some brother on Facebook urges the sisters to be a wee bit more intentional about modesty issues, and a lot more intentional about the wee bits of cloth they were attempting to call a swimsuit. The word *triggered* is way over-used these days, but modesty really is a subject that triggers a lot of people.

The fact that a simple call for modesty can be met with fits of rage, outbursts of vituperation, and explosive denunciations of rising legalism tells you a lot about how deep our cultural crater is.

So I said in my first letter that you should want to become the kind of woman that the kind of man you would want to marry would want to marry. That principle extends to this point.

Not to be mercenary, but women are attractive to men, and different things that women do are attractive to different kinds of men. If you dress like a tramp, or if (being a Christian) you lean just a little bit trampy, you will in fact get male attention. Unfortunately, however wreathed in smiles it might be, you are attracting the kind of man you should not want to attract. The kind of men who work hard to avoid being pigs will begin to work hard at avoiding you.

But this leads to a crucial distinction—a woman should of course want to be *attractive*, but she should want to accomplish this without *attracting.*

If she goes to the mall and by the time she gets to the far end she has a trail of about fifteen guys following her, then she is doing something seriously wrong. The distinction is this. An attractive woman is a lady, and a lady is a woman who comports herself *with self-respect.*

You should want "she is certainly attractive." You should not want "she is certainly an attraction."

An attracting woman is a public hazard, and is communicating that she is shameless and abandoned. She is lacking in self-respect, which is why she comes across like she is nothing more a female in heat. But when the rage machine starts in on this *common sense observation,* they want to distort the whole discussion—as though women were a monolithic group and all men were a monolithic group.

I saw one meme that put it this way: "Modesty isn't about covering up our bodies because they're bad, modesty is about justifying the poor behavior of men at the expense of women." Or here is another one: "When you call a woman a slut what you mean is someone who expresses her sexuality in a manner that does not meet your approval."

This kind of feminist impudence wants to say that a woman should be able to display herself in any fashion she wants to, and if men have a problem with that it is only because they are being pigs. But of course there are many men who are not pigs—they are the ones who steer clear of women like that. They steer clear because their mothers taught them to respect women—and that means staying away from women who refuse to respect themselves.

But then those women come to the conclusion that all men are pigs because that's the only kind they ever meet. "Where are all the decent men?"— the lament goes up from some dive bar. But they only meet the kind of men they do because of how they are baiting the trap. You can't set out a roach motel under your sink and then wonder why you aren't catching more trout.

The men who are *not* pigs are attracted to women who are characterized by dignity, self-respect, and class. Dress like the kind of person the kind of person you would want to marry would like you to dress. That kind of person wouldn't want you dressing that same disorderly way after you were married, right? Why would a decent husband want to go out in public with you in order to give all the low-lifes a treat?

So the kind of man you would want to marry should be the kind of man who would find you *attractive*, but who would be put off if you appeared to be wanting to *attract* all the sailors in the fleet.

And this demeanor is what the Bible calls women to cultivate. There are two significant components to feminine modesty. A biblically modest woman needs to avoid ostentatious display, and she needs to be aware of the need to maintain a real sense of sexual decorum. And she should recognize that *both* of these elements are, at the end of the day, sexual.

Wearing sexually provocative things—décolletage and so on—is obviously sexual, but so is the flamboyant campy stuff. When a woman wears outrageous clothing, even if everything is covered up, the subtext is that she must be some kind of super freak in bed. And Scripture tells Christian women to stay well away from both of these problems.

Allow me to quote a chain of passages, with a few comments here and there in between, and then I will try to roll them all up in a summary at the end—the kind of summary that might help you frame how you want to relate to the brothers in how you advertise. Yes, I know, I know—I used the word *advertise*. We'll get to that.

Just know for the present that women cannot help but advertise—it is yet another inescapable concept. *Not whether but which.* It is not whether you advertise, but which things you advertise. The biblical word for advertising is adorning.

> Whose adorning let it not be that outward adorning of plaiting the hair, and of wearing of gold, or of putting on of apparel; But let it be the hidden man of the heart, in that which is not corruptible, even the ornament of a meek and quiet spirit, which is in the sight of God of great price. For after this manner in the old time the holy women also, who trusted in

> God, adorned themselves, being in subjection unto
> their own husbands. (1 Pet. 3:3–5)

Peter says to focus on the inner woman, not on externals. A woman's beauty is supposed to be from inside out and not outside in. Notice that Peter is assuming that the women are adorning themselves, and he is instructing them *how* to adorn themselves. Notice also that a *man* is teaching them this.

Now some Christian traditions have taken this prohibition of women bespangling themselves as a requirement to be dour and straight-laced and fussy-faced and dowdy. A woman's make-up and hair ought not to serve the same function as flying buttresses, that function being to hold the cathedral up. Peter explicitly says that women should adorn themselves the same way that the holy women of old did. But the charge is that women should in fact be adorned. If a woman obeyed this passage, she would be a classy lady.

Paul, another man, says something similar.

> In like manner also, that women adorn themselves in modest apparel, with shamefacedness and sobriety; not with broided hair, or gold, or pearls, or costly array; But (which becometh women professing godliness) with good works. (1 Tim. 2:9–10)

Such women are not adorned china dolls. They are workers—given over to good works. They are dignified and sober. The archaic language of the KJV here may be misleading—shamefacedness means with propriety or decency or moderation. Again, they don't try to fix a restless spirit within by means of externals. For too many women, there is a correlation between how much attention they give to their external appearance and how spiritually insecure they are.

> Moreover the Lord says: "Because the daughters of Zion are haughty, and walk with outstretched necks and wanton eyes, walking and mincing as they go, making a jingling with their feet, therefore the Lord will strike with a scab the crown of the head of the daughters of Zion, and the Lord will uncover their secret parts." In that day the Lord will take away the finery: The jingling anklets, the scarves, and the crescents; the pendants, the bracelets, and the veils; the headdresses, the leg ornaments, and the headbands; the perfume boxes, the charms, and the rings; the nose jewels, the festal apparel, and the mantles; the outer garments, the purses, and the mirrors; the fine linen, the turbans, and the robes. And so it shall be: Instead of a sweet smell there will be a stench; instead of a sash, a rope; instead of well-set hair, baldness; instead of a rich robe, a girding of sackcloth; and branding instead of beauty. (Isa. 3:16–24, NKJV)

There are many articles of clothing described
here in Isaiah, but the thing that sets the tone is
right near the top of the list—wanton eyes. The
wanton eyes create the meaning of everything else.
The wanton eyes set the tone. This is the super freak
aspect I mentioned earlier. And it should be mentioned that too many Christian women think that
they can do everything else that pagan women do,
and then just leave out the wanton eyes part. The
reason this doesn't work is that the tone is already
set, the meaning of everything is already assigned.

> For at the window of my house I looked through
> my casement, and beheld among the simple ones,
> I discerned among the youths, a young man void
> of understanding, passing through the street near
> her corner; and he went the way to her house, in
> the twilight, in the evening, in the black and dark
> night: And, behold, there met him a woman with
> the attire of an harlot, and subtil of heart. (She
> is loud and stubborn; Her feet abide not in her
> house: Now is she without, now in the streets, and
> lieth in wait at every corner.) So she caught him,
> and kissed him, and with an impudent face said
> unto him, I have peace offerings with me; This day
> have I payed my vows. Therefore came I forth to
> meet thee, diligently to seek thy face, and I have
> found thee. I have decked my bed with coverings
> of tapestry, with carved works, with fine linen of
> Egypt. I have perfumed my bed with myrrh, aloes,

and cinnamon. Come, let us take our fill of love until the morning: Let us solace ourselves with loves. For the goodman is not at home, he is gone a long journey: He hath taken a bag of money with him, and will come home at the day appointed. With her much fair speech she caused him to yield, with the flattering of her lips she forced him. He goeth after her straightway, as an ox goeth to the slaughter, or as a fool to the correction of the stocks; Till a dart strike through his liver; as a bird hasteth to the snare, and knoweth not that it is for his life. (Prov. 7:6–23)

This particular seduction is overtly a trap, and it is a trap that will cost this young chump his life. We know it is a trap because she "lieth in wait." She has baited the hook appropriately—the "attire of an harlot." Her heart has twists and turns in it, and her tongue is one that flatters.

You should want to *be* a godly Christian woman, and consequently you should want to *look* like one. This means that modesty has to be treated like the feminine virtue it is, and not as a laugh line. This modesty does not mean dowdy, because Christian women are to strive to be adorned. But this kind of modesty does mean that you should aspire to be a class act.

And this brings me to one last comment. Don't think of this in terms of whether or not an article of clothing is going to "stumble the brothers." This particular deflection is misleading. When guys stumble, they stumble into lusting after. When women stumble, they stumble into wanting to *be* lusted after. Guys do have a desire to turn and gawk, and the guys who are working on not being pigs actively mortify that desire. Don't make those guys avoid you. Girls have a desire to turn heads, and so that is the desire you must mortify. If you do that, you do well. This means that if you avoid stumbling *yourself,* the brothers will probably be fine.

Your uncle,
Douglas

THREE

ON GUARDING YOUR HEART

Dear Darla,

So I think the next issue I would like to cover, if you would be so kind as to keep on reading, is the importance of guarding your heart. That is simple enough to say, but actually doing it can be quite the challenge.

You were brought up in a biblical home, and you have a really good relationship with your dad, I am happy to note, and so this will be easier for you than it is for many girls. But you will still have to be intentional about it. You cannot do this on cruise control. It is not something that happens all by itself. In fact, when left all to itself, the opposite thing happens.

Precisely because you have a commitment to traditional roles for men and women, you know that the man is expected to take the initiative in a relationship, and the woman is expected to be the one who responds to him. She ought not be the one who asks him out on a date, for example, and she ought not to be the one who proposes. So far so good. But there are ways that you could "initiate" something, even if it is just going on in your head, that can cause no little difficulty for you.

So imagine two lines down the middle of the room, and we have all the guys on the far side of one of the lines, and all the girls on the far side of the other one. Nobody is in between the two lines, and we will call that the zone of vulnerability. Getting into the zone of vulnerability means that if you get into the zone you can't get out of the zone without getting hurt.

But it is not as though living in the zone is a bad place to be—every married couple lives there, for example. That zone is not a prohibited zone, but God has said that He doesn't want us living there unprotected or unsecured. That is what the covenant does; that is what wedding rings do. When a couple is shacked up together for a few years, and then they break up, all you have is a divorce without the attorney's fees. But the emotional and spiritual damage are not dependent on the fact of attorney's fees.

When you fail to guard your heart, what is happening is that you are drifting into the zone. Now this can happen overtly, when a guy and a girl are being stupid, and they are in a dating relationship for five years. If you do that, there is no way to stay out of the zone, and we probably ought not to say that they were "drifting" into the zone. It was more like the zone was a pool, and they were cannonballing into the deep end of it.

But a girl in your position is more likely to *drift* into the zone. This can happen different ways. First, it can happen inside your head through daydreaming. Say an eligible young man starts attending your church, and he joins your college and career group. Ten of the young women can start imagining all sorts of possibilities for him, and four of those young women *talk* about those possibilities for him that they have imagined. You can think that their conversation is tedious and silly, and still be affected by it. "What if he. . ." Imagining all sorts of scenes and scenarios would be an example of not guarding your heart. If he asks another girl out, and you are disappointed but shake it off in half an hour, you are doing fine. If he does that and you are devastated, that means you daydreamed yourself into the zone. And there is an in-between. Say you are not devastated, but you are certainly more disappointed than you ought to have been, and the half hour is more like a week . . . that's something you really want to avoid in the future. So guard your heart by guarding your imagination.

Incidentally, one way of guarding your imagination is to monitor your consumption of romance novels and/or Rom-Com chick flicks. I am not saying that they *have* to be considered sinful (although some of them are), but a steady diet of them is nothing more than pornography for the emotions. And just like sexual porn, it distorts your understanding of the world. All it will do is make your heart goopy, and it is really hard to guard a goopy heart.

You want to be *preparing* your heart for when the right guy shows up, and that means you must *guard* your heart until he does.

But let us grant that the reason you don't want to guard your heart is that not guarding it is, for the moment, *fun*. Or consoling. Or reassuring. Or fun. That is, it is fun until it crashes.

Another way to drift into the zone is to have a circle of friends that you get very comfortable with—they are like a pair of your favorite slippers. Life is easy around them. There are three guys in this group and three girls. You get along well, and you do lots of fun things together, and nobody is dating exactly, but you do see each other three or four times a week. Movies at somebody's apartment. Frisbee golf. Ice cream socials at the church. You are "the gang." At some point, some of you are going to start drawing invisible lines above your heads, and that creates invisible expectations in your hearts—the ones you are not guarding.

Say you are particularly good friends with one of the guys, and the formal status that you and everybody else have assigned to this relationship is that you are "just friends." That's all you could ever be, right? That is because nobody has said or done anything romantic. But you *are* close to him, closer than a brother. And one day, when the two of you are having coffee at some joint—and it is not a date—he says something like, "Look, just thought I'd check . . . we're just friends, right?"

What are you going to do then? What can you do? You are not in any position to stand up at your table, bosom heaving, in order to cry out, "No, no, Trevor! Let me bear your children!" Suppose you realized in that moment that you had indeed fallen for him, and *he* had just gotten confirmation from you that you were "just friends." And believe me, many guys are stupid enough, even the smart ones, to think that having had such a conversation settles a matter like that.

This is a controversial subject for some, but you would be right to gather from what I have written that I believe that one-on-one male/female friendships are not a possibility. At the very least, it is a safe bet for you to act as though they are not a possibility.

You might ask how you were supposed to guard your heart in circumstances like that. The answer is simple, but it is only simple if you act early enough, and set your standards in place before you are maneuvered into places that are pleasant enough going in, but which leave you hurt or devastated going out. Such places are called the zone of vulnerability.

Stay away from set groups that have even numbers of guys and girls. You want the gang to have five guys, three girls. Four girls, two guys. And in such groups don't get so used to your friends there that you think you can just go to coffee with one of the guys and have it "not be a date." Of course it is date. The fact that a guy and girl are industriously pretending to themselves that it is not a date doesn't keep it from being a date.

Neither does it keep things from being sexually charged, incidentally. This is how "hookups" *can* happen between Christians, incidentally. They know they are not "in a relationship," and so they hang on to that fact tenaciously, but this does not erase the sexual energy that both are carefully suppressing—until it explodes.

So how do you stay out of situations like that? Well, you do it by saying, "No, thank you." He will be puzzled and say, "You don't want a coffee?" And then you would say that you wouldn't mind a coffee, but that you have a policy against spending any one-on-one time with guys. And he will be shocked and flabbergasted and all that. And he will say that all he wanted was to talk with you about something that happened to him that day, and how's he supposed to do that? And then you would say that he could ask you on a date, and you would be happy to check with your dad. And then just look at him with a fat face.

What you are doing is refusing to get maneuvered into a nebulous relationship. If you are on a date, you are on a date, and you both know it. You don't want to be sitting in some coffee bar while wondering to yourself, "What *is* this? Where *are* we?"

You should also have a policy against guys coming into your apartment if no one else is there. You have standards that you have set beforehand and you simply apply them. What this means is that you *respect* yourself. You are not unattainable, but you should *seem* unattainable to the guys.

Out in the pagan world, where men and women hang out together, and the ethical barriers are down, the women are easy. This is one of the reasons the men don't commit. They are willing to *use* easy women, but they don't want to *commit* to easy women.

The Christian version of this avoids the immorality (for the most part), but many times the girls make the mistake of being *emotionally* easy. And then the same thing happens on that level. They get emotionally used, and the men still don't commit. The guys like talking to pretty girls, because who wouldn't? They need someone to pour out their troubles to, and mom's not there.

You know this kind of thing is going on in the gang, for example, if a girl cleans up a guy's apartment for him. Or if she takes it upon herself to cook a birthday cake for one of the guys. Or runs errands for him. Don't be that girl. It's low-rent.

To repeat, you are not unattainable, but you want it to seem that way. This is not being snooty or snobbish. When it comes to one-on-one relationships with guys—I exclude your father and brothers and cousin—you should have too much self respect to drift into a place where you are emotionally available to men who have made no promises. You will spare yourself a lot of grief.

The last thing is this. Being able to do this is only possible if you are walking with God. The idea of "guarding your heart" refers to this vertical relationship with Him primarily, walking in the path of wisdom: "Keep thy heart with all diligence; For out of it are the issues of life" (Prov. 4:23).

The issues of life really do flow out of this. If you are walking with God, if you are close to your dad, if you honor your mother and imitate her, and *if you listen to your uncle*, your life will be pleasant in the land the Lord your God is giving to you.

Your uncle,
Douglas

FOUR

UNDERSTANDING GUYS

Dear Darla,

In order to interact with guys generally, in order to date one of them, and in order to marry one, it is highly recommended that you have some understanding of what you are getting into.

Now in order to explain to you what you are getting into, I am going to have to generalize. There is nothing wrong with this, so long as you realize that there *are* exceptions, and that life is not always tidy, and you should not clutch at any generalization, however accurate it might be, as though it were a theorem out of Euclid about triangles having three sides. Triangles always have three sides. Guys are not *always* the way I will describe for you, but they are *usually* that way. So budget for exceptions, while at the same time expecting my descriptions to come true, right before your very eyes.

Guys are simple, in a way that women are not. Consequently, you will be tempted to over-analyze everything, and you are accustomed to things being complicated. You have adjusted to those complications, and you think they are normal. You think that guys are doing the same thing. You analyze his brief comment, that comment with a thousand possible meanings, when it was just a brief comment.

When I say that guys are simple, I am not saying that they are stupid. They are very intelligent, and can win wars, and send people to the moon, and build smart phones, and so on. But their intelligence rides on a very different operating platform than your intelligence does. As a general rule, guys think about one thing at a time, like a dog pushing a rock up and down the sidewalk. Breakfast, breakfast, commute, commute, work, work, work, work, work, lunch, lunch, work, work, work, work, work, commute, commute, dinner, dinner, tv, tv, sleep, sleep, repeat, repeat. If you ask them to do more than the one thing they are currently occupied with doing, it annoys them.

Women can generally do three things at a time, think about two things, talk on the phone about another thing, and all with a baby on their hip. This is a grand mystery, but it is also how the meat loaf, and peas, and mashed potatoes all arrive at the table at the same time, all of them hot.

Now in the examples I used above, I was assuming a married couple. But suppose you have these two different ways of thinking still single and in the process of getting together. Think of this as a divine sense of humor thing. They will both have very different perceptions of what the heck is going on.

When a man decides it is time to court or pursue a woman, he is doing "the next thing." He knows he needs to be married, and so it goes on his to-do list. Men think in a linear way, one thing at a time. Women are lateral thinkers, and can run multiple tracks at once. One of your problems will be that of assuming that he is doing the same thing that you would be doing when he is doing nothing of the kind. You will be like a master chess player in a game with a novice, and when the novice makes some random move, you will think of three different ways that *could* be an uncanny genius move. But it isn't. It is simply what he did, and it seemed like a good idea to him at the time.

If it is outside their realm of experience, the fact that men are such narrow, linear thinkers can be mistaken for stupidity—or malevolence. You bring up something perfectly reasonable, like the fact that he asked you out on the three-month anniversary of your first date, to the *day*, which you thought was *so sweet*, and he just blinks at you dumbfounded. He actually asked you out because you already went out on Monday, and Friday comes after Monday. That anniversary thought never entered his head, and not only so, but it never occurred to him that such a thought could ever enter *anyone's* head.

So one of the things you will have to get used to is the fact that heterosexual relationships are always cross-cultural, bilingual situations. You come from different worlds. He's a guy. They do things differently over there. You must make room for that. Do not make the mistake of expecting him to make room for the way you are, while at the same time not making room for the way he is. Meet in the middle. That's what sensible people do.

Now if I were giving advice to him I would be saying the same thing. He needs to become bilingual also. He needs to make room for the way women are, and stop doing certain things. Give and take, give and take. For example, throw a bunch of guys together in a group—military unit, hunting party, bowling team, etc.—and one of the ways they will bond is by making fun of each other. They are not being awful. They are making friends. And some men make the mistake of trying this out on a girl they are dating. This is not generally done by guys with sisters, but it is done. So if you don't want a guy who makes this kind of mistake, don't be the kind of girl who makes this mistake.

Another difference—one that has some relevance to the challenge of getting together—is that men and women are attracted to different *initial* things. I emphasize that word *initial* because I am not saying that other traits are unimportant to men and to women—far from it. But men are attracted initially by *looks*, and women are attracted initially by *status*.

You have to make adjustments for age and station, but the principle is the same all the way up. In high school, she is pretty and he is the quarterback. Twenty years later, she is attractive and he is a CEO. Complain about this all you want, it is not going to go away.

This is why a young man has to be *taught* that looks aren't everything. He will tempted to see that she is really pretty and stop there, asking no more questions. But he needs to be encouraged to go on to the issues of character, brains, and work ethic. Hollywood is full of beauties that nobody can seem to remain married to: "Charm is deceitful and beauty is passing, but a woman who fears the Lord, she shall be praised" (Prov. 31:30, NKJV).

Let me illustrate this principle with a couple in a lousy marriage. Let's say that the marriage has been bad for a few years, they just had an argument, and then he goes off to work. Now let's say that on that day, some other woman at work makes a pass at him. Because he is vulnerable, and provided she is attractive, he doesn't even need to know her name in order to be tempted. He is attracted physically first, and then after that he can get as emotionally entangled as anyone. But it is sexual first. In the meantime, back at home, the wife is vulnerable just like he is—but not the same way. If the UPS guy tried something ("hey, baby"), he would get the door slammed in his face, no matter how bad the marriage was. But the next door neighbor, the one who helped her get the patio furniture in when it rained, and who took a moment to chat with her over the back fence that other time, and who seemed like he was really listening, etc. . . . She will be tempted also, but not right away, and it will be emotionally first, and physically later. She is vulnerable if he seems like a successful guy, and if, *as* that successful guy, he notices her.

Okay, back to singles. The point there is men and women respond to different initial prompts. There is nothing wrong with those initial prompts in themselves, but it is a drastic mistake to limit yourself to them. Men and women both need to look past status, looks, and personality, and ask the really serious questions about *character.*

A girl can be pretty and pleasant, and still be an airhead. Having breakfast with an airhead would get old pretty quick. A man can be an alpha, really going places, and be a suffocating presence wherever he lives. That would get old even quicker.

But beware of the real threat—a man can also be a mousy beta, coming up with new and timid ways of abdicating every single day, and that would be the worst. If a man is being a pencil neck, it should not matter to you that his pastor told him it was servant leadership, and to keep on deferring. You should have nothing to do with him—although you may feel sorry for him. He was diffident to begin with, and then his pastors spent years teaching him that his timidity was some kind of an aphrodisiac. Feel sorry for him, but move on. You should want a man that you believe is fully capable of taking you on. And if you are a handful, then he needs to be a masculine handful.

I am talking about first impressions. You will notice, *first*, whether he is sending the appropriate signals that indicate he will be able to *provide* and *protect*. Is he a hard worker? Does he have a job? Is he strong? Is he courageous? Do other men respect him? There is nothing wrong with you noticing such things first, and not responding to him unless you have noticed them. They should be on your list.

And there is nothing wrong with him asking you out because he thought you were cute. But there is a hazard in being cute, as you almost certainly know. When you are being cute, more guys notice than just the one you noticed. So don't get irritated when you get unwanted attention. It is part of the cost of doing business.

When a guy you are not interested in asks you out, you must receive it and respond to it as a compliment. *That is what it is.* You should graciously and kindly decline the compliment, but this is possible to do while treating it *as* a compliment. Some women are guilty of a great unkindness by treating an invitation from an undesired male as "creepy," while at the same time treating similar behavior from a desired male as "so sweet." Say that the undesired male compliments how you look, and asks you out. Your response should be warm and firm. "I really appreciate the compliment, but no thank you." The mere fact of the attention is never creepy—although the manner of it could be. If a man is rude, then you may respond to the rudeness. But he is not being rude for noticing what you were wishing that other guy would notice.

If the right kind of guy saw you on the subway, somehow tracked you down on Facebook, and showed up at your church the following Sunday, why is this material for a sweet Rom-Com, and not the material for a thriller stalker movie?

Here's another important difference between guys and girls. If you don't want attention from a particular guy, and you decline to go out with him, *do not give any reasons* other than the fact that you do not wish to go. This is because guys like obstacle courses. If you give a reason, they will treat that as an invitation to start running the obstacle course. "No, thank you. I'm busy Friday night." All you are doing is inviting the follow-up question, which is, "What about Saturday night?" So if a guy is persistent, you need to say something like, "I am appreciative of the attention, but I would prefer to keep our relationship as it is. But thank you for the compliment."

There are other aspects to all of this which I am
sure we will get to, but that should suffice for the
moment.

Your uncle,
Douglas

FIVE

ON NOT BEING CATTY ABOUT IT

Dear Darla,

I told you in my last letter that guys are pretty straightforward. This is not to say that there are no complicated men, for there are, but taking one thing with another, guys are less complex than women. It can take a women some adjusting to get used to this, because underneath each simple action he takes or simple word he utters, she suspects deeper forces at work. Consequently, men can be hard for women to understand because they represent an alien thought form.

But women can be hard for women to understand as well, and this is for the old-fashioned reason—the complexity. Some of the complexity that
women exhibit is easy for other women to follow
because it is their native language. They see and
understanding what is happening. But some of a
woman's complexity is as hard for another woman
to follow as it is difficult for the men to follow. It is a
masked complexity.

This usually happens when sin gets into the picture, and the sin I am talking about is usually the
sin of envy or striving. When it breaks out in a circle
of women who are friends, classmates, roommates,
or acquaintances, it comes out in the form of cattiness. Now the Bible doesn't really talk about cattiness, but it does talk about envy.

> A sound heart is the life of the flesh: *But envy the*
> *rottenness of the bones."* (Prov. 14:30)

> Being filled with all unrighteousness, fornication,
> wickedness, covetousness, maliciousness; *full of*
> *envy,* murder, debate, deceit, malignity; whisper-
> ers. (Rom. 1:29, emphasis added)

Envy is no good, and it frequently comes out
in the form of cattiness. And cattiness is a sin that
makes everyone wonder afterwards, "Where did
that come from?"

Now I want you recognize that I am going to be generalizing again. No doubt you will able to think of exceptions to what I am about to say—I certainly can. But nevertheless, the exceptions should not prevent you from using these generalization to navigate some complex situations. There is safety to be found in these generalizations.

You might be wondering—when you wrote and asked about relationships with guys—why I have veered off and am talking about relationships with your friends and roommates. The reason is this. There is something about girls you will have to understand if you want to know about guys. And that is the fact that the other girls are really interested in your interest in guys. And there are landmines there.

Guys are competitive, and will compete over anything. This can get tedious for the sisters, but one advantage it has is that they are accustomed to competing. They compete over who can throw the rock farthest into the river, they compete about who got to church first, they compete about whose birthday came first in the year, and so on. Guys compete, and they are pretty good at taking it all in stride. They all know the rules.

The girls are not competitive in the same way. They don't turn everything into a competition. "Ha ha! I finished my book first!" Girls are not ready to compete at the drop of a hat . . . unless they are competing over a guy . . . or guys. When it comes to the guys, everything tends to reduce to a competition. Hair, clothes, makeup, jewelry, and so on. Women are very competitive when it comes to masculine attention. Sometimes we think that women are not competitive because their lives are one great big competition.

You can see this unfolding when a new guy shows up in your community. There is a tendency with the women, some openly and some more discretely, to start posting up under the basket. This first reaction is a carnal one—nothing spiritual about it. But the thing that is carnal is not that you want to make a good first impression on the new guy. That by itself is fine. The problem is what happens when you are doing it in a crowd, and the thing has become competitive. The problem is identified in the desire to start throwing elbows.

This is worth isolating. If you were a rancher's daughter out on a remote spread in the hinterlands of Montana, and a friend of your brother from college came to visit, there would be absolutely nothing wrong with you trying to look nice for the visitor. I am not talking about trying to look attractive when it is lawful and right for you to want to be attractive. I will get to that in my next letter. For the present, I am talking about collisions with the other sisters. I am especially talking about inexplicable collisions with the other sisters. I am talking about the dynamics of envy.

Envy is a sin that must be mortified, and for women the sin is much more likely to arise when you envy another woman's success with a guy, or with the guys, or when you are peeved at her transparent attempts to be catty with you.

This is a sin that is sinful right on the surface, but it is also a sin that rests upon a deep doctrinal foundation. Let's start with that foundation, and then move on to what it means to mortify the sin of envious striving.

God has laid out a purpose and plan for your life. We are God's workmanship, created in Christ Jesus to do good works, which God prepared beforehand for us to do (Eph. 2:10). The good works He has prepared for you include your children, and their names, and *their father's name.* And when it comes to such things, God never double books. This means that this guy, whoever he is, cannot be the Lord's will for more than one of you—and maybe he is the Lord's will for less than one of you. No one has decretal dibs.

Now if you are not right for him, then he most certainly is not right for you. It is never a perfect match in one direction, and a mismatch in the other. When mismatched couples marry, and it does happen, the result is a trial for both of them, and not just one of them.

The exhortation therefore is *to trust God.* If you are invited to be a bridesmaid in yet another stupid wedding, you need to rest in Him, trust Him, rely on Him. Now I am talking to you this way because I am in the highest degree confident that you are going to be married in the foreseeable future. But there are women who very much want to be married, and no one suitable has approached them, and they are getting on in years. That is for a separate letter also.

Right now I am talking about a cluster of girls who are all going to get married. Now if they all get married, it is going to happen in a particular order. Somebody is going to be first, and somebody is going to be last. If you are settled on the doctrinal point, getting married to the right man is far more important than getting married first, or early in the line-up. But if you have given way to envy and striving, it is going to be possible to start making poor decisions.

Now there are some girls who are pretty steady, and I rank you among them, and they are not prone to the sin of competing with the other girls over the guys. But this by itself won't keep you out of snarls. Suppose that there is a girl in your circles who *is* prone to envy. She identified herself in this way when you went out and bought a cute blouse, and two days later she came home with the same one. This was not an accident.

So suppose this guy shows up, and you are not interested. Nevertheless, she starts competing like crazy with you. This is when the inexplicable cattiness enters. She starts making snide comments and odd comparisons. As soon as you figure out what is going on, there will be a temptation to think, "You know, I don't really want to compete with her over him, but if I were to do so, I would *win*, darn it." That is the sinful part. That is the part that must be mortified.

Your uncle,
Douglas

SIX

ON AVOIDING ROMANTIC REVERIE

Dear Darla,

In my last letter I talked about the surreptitious competition that women tend to engage in, as opposed to the "out in the open" competition that is preferred by men. Men tend to compete about everything, women included, while women tend to compete over men, in a way that extends into everything.

Not only is this the case, but there are gradations to that surreptitious competition. Take a hypothetical case, the one I used earlier. Say that an eligible bachelor moves into your community, into your circle. One of the first things that people do is that they start matchmaking in their heads, and they start doing this almost immediately.

This can be done in a way that exhibits really bad manners, and it can be done in a way characterized by modesty and good taste—but it is going to be done. All the older church ladies immediately begin wondering if "he would be good for . . ." The bad manners come in when they start wondering this out loud, or if they fail to give the young gentleman a minute to unpack his suitcase.

The younger women do the same thing, but will usually be more reticent to talk too much about it— because their circle of friends includes others who might be lining up the options differently. "I hope he gets to meet Suzy Q. . ." That is less likely to be said if you are present and you are not Suzie Q. And of course, it might be said, and loudly, if you are present and you are Suzie Q's main rival.

Now all of this can be done in a way that is gossipy and wrong, and done by people who seem to think that pairing people off is the most important thing that God assigned to us in this life, which is not the case. But meeting members of the opposite sex is one of the more important things we do, and for those who are in your age group, it should be one of the top three.

Nothing is served by pretending that this is not the case. If an activity is inevitable, then we should be trying to figure out how to do it biblically and well, which is quite a different thing than pretending that it can't be happening because we think that somehow it ought not to be happening.

So the trick is to do this intelligently, without investing all sorts of emotional capital into it. In other words, you do not want to start daydreaming—you are evaluating whether or not a man could be a good fit, and not running headlong into a romantic reverie.

But here is the thing. This temptation is likely to come from outside you, from your circle of friends, and if you are not guarding the combustible materials in your heart, you are setting yourself up for some real grief. You do not want to be Marianne in *Sense and Sensibility*, but rather Elinor.

Excitements are contagious, and if your friends are all in a doodah over the arrival of whoever this guy is, and if two of them have nominated you for the lead role when it comes to attempts on capturing his heart, you might be tempted to remain placid on the surface, but to give way to woolgathering in the midnight hours. That kind of thing is really unfruitful. If you don't have anything to go on, don't go on.

Daydreaming is occurring when you skip over certain preliminary things, like him actually showing an interest, or him exhibiting the kind of character that would make it wise for you even to be interested, and, having skipped over those things (to be "settled" later), you find yourself thinking about the wedding day, or a honeymoon in the Bahamas.

The whole situation is taking shape in a competitive environment, even though not everyone is competing the same way. Think of it this way—there are the players competing on the court, there are different teams, there are the players on the bench who go in and play periodically, and then there are the season ticket holders at court side, playing vicariously. These people sitting court side could well be running various kinds of proxy wars—she is not after this guy herself, but she wants her friend to have a shot at him, and not you. And that is why that snide comment was made at church two weeks ago. She had never been rude to you before.

Now your responsibility in this kind of situation is to always *act, never react.* You should want to act on principle, and not to be reacting to circumstances. And because you are the woman, your range of activity when it comes to how you "act" is going to be fairly limited. You don't get to ask him out, in other words.

But even though you don't ask him out, you have every right to be in places where he is likely to be—just so long as it does not look like you are in hot pursuit. In other words, if he goes to the early service, there is no problem with you going to the early service too. These things happen. You are not stalking, or chasing, or taking the initiative. You are simply giving him the opportunity to initiate, if he so desires. But if he is taking a welding class at the community college, and you take up a sudden interest in welding, finding it *fascinating*, then that would be rhetorically problematic.

But prior to all of this should be the thoughtful, prayerful deliberation about the characteristics of the kind of man you would like to marry. You can do this with no bachelors in sight, and you can do this if a candidate has appeared on the horizon. You are not out of line to ask yourself questions about a particular guy. This is due diligence. It is a godly activity. It is not ridiculous, and you are not being brazen. This is all between you and God, remember?

Most of your responsible actions will be centered on how you *think* of him, and what you allow your emotions to consequently do. You want to think like a godly Christian woman, one who has a godly set of Christian priorities.

So if you are avoiding daydreams, and if you are avoiding bad manners (e.g. where you were the one who made the rude comment at church), then you are simply being a responsible Christian woman. Make a list. Describe the kind of man you would be interested in. Share it with no one, except perhaps your mom or dad. Pray through it. Feel free to make adjustments as you learn more.

You are making a working list, not pouring a concrete foundation. What sorts of things should be on the list? Well, that is largely up to you, but here are some suggestions. Some would be obligatory for any intelligent Christian woman, while others would be a matter of personal preference.

Is he Reformed? Is he a reader? What kind of a work ethic does he have? Do the other men look up to him? Is he taller than you? Is he athletic? Could he serve as an elder in the church some day? Does his family have a similar culture to your family? What is his view on Ephesians 5? And so on.

And, of course, you should do this realistically, remembering what I have mentioned before. A man who fit the description of this list is a man who could well have a list of his own. How would you do with regard to that list?

> For I say, through the grace given unto me, to every man that is among you, not to think of himself more highly than he ought to think; but to think soberly, according as God hath dealt to every man the measure of faith. (Rom. 12:3)

Your uncle,
Douglas

SEVEN

STAYING OUT OF CARTOON WORLD

Dear Darla,

Okay, so now we are getting into some treacherous territory. This is an area fraught with peril, and one of the reasons it is so perilous is that we all, for emotional reasons, have decided to ignore and suppress a major facet of male/female interactions. The end result is that nobody knows what is going on. Everybody's doing it, but nobody is paying attention to it.

Now assume that you have a room full of young men and young women, all unattached. It is a social event, a mixer of some kind. For the purposes of this thought experiment, let us assume that character issues are equally important to everyone—nobody wants to marry a bum, a dirtbag, or a harlot. So the character issues are fixed—everybody there is going to Heaven when they die.

Just because everyone is exhibiting godly character does not mean that any given couple would be a good match. There are all sorts of additional variables in play. You couldn't just pair everybody off randomly and have happy things result. Godly character is a necessary condition for a good marriage, but it is not a sufficient condition. What this means is that character is essential. If you don't have it, you cannot have a good marriage. But a sufficient condition is stronger than that. If you have the sufficient conditions met, you *will* have a good marriage. Character is necessary, but not sufficient.

Now hold that thought because I am going to jump to Scripture for a second. But in order to make this point, I am going to need to qualify it first. All of us are told to love our neighbor as we do ourselves (Lev. 19:18), and we are also taught that our neighbor is whatever person happens to be in front of us at the moment (Luke 10:33). This means that husband and wife are included in the command to love one another (John 13:34). In addition, all of us are told to honor all men (1 Pet. 2:17). This respect, this honor that we are to render is not attached to the sex of the recipient. This means that husband

and wife are included in the command to respect everyone. Everyone loves and everyone respects. This is straightforward. Husbands should of course love and respect their wives. Wives should of course respect and love their husbands.

But the word order there matters. When Scriptures focuses on the *particular* duties of husbands to wives, the emphasis is on love. Husbands, love your wives as Christ loved the church and gave Himself for it (Eph. 5:25, 33). And when Scripture addresses wives *as wives*, it tells them to honor and respect their husbands (Eph. 5:22, 24, 33).

The central husbandly duty is to love. The central wifely duty is to respect. The New Testament nowhere commands wives to love their husbands. Now it is certainly okay. It is not a sin to love your husband. There is one place in Titus where the older women are to teach the younger women to be husband-lovers (Tit. 2:4), but the word there is a compound word (*philandros*), which I would render as "into husband" and "into kids" (*philoteknos*). In a word, domestic and enjoying it.

But when a wife is being encouraged to focus on her wifely responsibility, Scripture tells her to focus on respect. Now you are a single woman, and so why am I telling you this? The reason is that what you will be commanded to do with regard to your future husband, whoever he is, should be something you take into account when you are evaluating different men as possible candidates for that position. You should, in a word, be asking yourself if respecting such a man would be easy, challenging, or impossible.

Remember that we are not talking about character only. That is included, but we are talking about more than that. A man might be a godly man, and yet impossible for you to look up to. And not to put too fine a point on it, that would be a bad match. We are not gnostics. What if you are a lot smarter than he is?

You should be asking yourself if respect comes naturally, easily. If you marry such a man, there will still be times when submission is still a real challenge—so don't make it harder on yourself than it needs to be. A wise Puritan once said to the men that they must choose their love, and then love their choice.

It is the same for you, only different. You must choose your head, and then obey your head. It is legitimate for you to go back and forth in your mind about it now because you have no covenantal obligation to this man or that man. But you ought to run thought experiments.

Ask yourself. "What if Henry, or John, or Mike wanted me to do something I really didn't want to do?" You are asking yourself if his pickup truck has the horsepower to pull your trailer.

All of this is related to something called hypergamy. This is a term from the social sciences and refers to "marrying up." Hypergamy is when someone

marries or forms a sexual relationship with someone of a superior educational or social background.
What I have been talking about from Scripture refers to the internal mechanism of all this—hypergamy that is sincere and heartfelt, in other words.
Someone who is simply ambitious could "marry
up" while personally despising the person they
married. The Eagles sang about that in "Lyin' Eyes,"
I believe. But a Christian woman should be hypergamous from the heart.

Given the way God made the world, hypergamy
is usually pursued and practiced by women. And
because women are created to respect their husbands in this way, they *want* to marry up.

Now men will often joke about their supposed
hypergamy, and while the occasional joke in this
vein might be fine, as a routine or standing joke
it is not a good idea. Men *think* they are telling a
self-deprecating joke. "I married a truly remarkable
woman who in the course of her life has had only
one notable lapse of judgment." Like I said, the
men think this is self-deprecating, but if women
as a class are far more hypergamous than the men
are, the joke is actually at their wife's expense. "In
the competition between women for a prize male,
a mate to be proud of, my wife came up short. My
wife is the loser wife. You see the results before
you." Wives *want* to be proud of their husbands,
they *want* to look up to them, and they don't need

their husbands joking around about what blundering oafs they are.

You have a wonderful relationship with your father. As you look around at the young men who might someday approach you, compare them to him. Don't compare them unfairly—budget for the years of experience and that sort of thing, but ask yourself if this young man is the kind of man that your father would have befriended when your father was that age. Is he the right caliber?

One last thing. The propaganda machinery of our age is constantly cudgeling us to prevent us from talking this way. They can't stop us from *behaving* this way, but they can succeed in confusing us, and they can make us flinch internally whenever someone states the obvious out loud. I once saw a feminist actress complaining about all the movies she had seen where a man and a woman get into a tight spot, and then the woman says something like, "What do we do now?" This was an offense not to be borne, an offense against feminist dogma, even though it is true to life and happens all the time. This actress did not complain about all the movies she had seen where a petite little kick-boxer lady took out five or six 200-pound thugs. That kind of egalitarianism only works in cartoon world.

Your uncle,
Douglas

EIGHT

LAWS OF ATTRACTION

Dear Darla,

So let's get down to the business of serious analysis. What are you looking for in a man? Because there is no man on the scene right now, this question of serious analysis, though you are thinking about the "qualities of a man you would want," is actually a question of serious self-analysis. You can't analyze him because he's not here yet.

You can come up with a list of characteristics and qualities, and you can write them down. Go ahead and do that. If something comes to mind, put it down. Make a stream of consciousness list. Just put it down. You can edit later, and you can prune things from the list later, and you can change things on the list later. This is a working draft. You are not examining a man, but rather examining yourself.

Now suppose you made such a list, and then a guy comes along who checks all the boxes. Suppose he takes you out a few times, and you decline going out with him a third time. Why? You just weren't feeling it. This is certainly your prerogative, and nobody's arguing that you should continue to go out with a guy just because he matches somebody else's list. But if he checks all the boxes on your list, and you still want to say no, this is only because you didn't put enough boxes on your list. Put those boxes on there now. If you said no because you wouldn't have checked those boxes had they been on your list, then put them on your list now so that you can refuse to check them. Then he will *not* be one who "checked all the boxes."

But before you say *no* to too many guys, it would perhaps be best if you analyzed your list. Is your list carnal? "I want a guy who is tall, dark, rich, and Reformed."

Is your list realistic? In other words, do you not know what league you are in? Would a guy who fit the description on your list be interested in you? The guy who matches your list is a guy who presumably has a list of his own. Are you on that list? We have touched on this before. You don't want an unrealistic list made up as a composite of the last ten Rom-Coms you watched.

This next question needs a bit more unpacking. Is your list disingenuous? What I mean by this is—"how brutally honest is your list?" Did you put things on your list, not because you find them attractive, but because you have been taught that you are *supposed* to find them attractive?

Let me give you a hypothetical example. Suppose there is a guy in your circle of friends who is sweet, humble, sacrificial, gentle, soft-spoken, and is a guy who will one day make the best deacon in the whole world. You like him fine, and don't object to his presence in the group, but the thought of going out with him produces a *meh* reaction in you. Now imagine another guy in the group who is kind of brash, talks too much in Bible studies, laughs a little too loudly, always seems to be in the center of whatever the action is, and the girls talk about him as kind of a pest. But he is not really maladroit— just too far out there for some people's taste. They talk about him too, and you agree with those comments, and you shake your head at the same things your friends shake their heads at. And yet, in unguarded moments, you find yourself thinking about how you could help fix him. Fix him is too strong. Help him. Tame him. Take the rough edges off him. Maybe a little sandpaper and deep red cherry stain.

What is going on here is that you find his masculinity attractive, but are not in a position to admit to yourself that you actually do find it attractive. You are not supposed to, according to our current societal conventions, and so you don't. He is putting dents in various social norms, and you feel like you have to *tsk* along with everybody else, and so you do.

In Scripture, men are told to love their wives, and so the smart men are looking for someone they think they could love. Women are told to respect their husbands, and so the smart women are looking for someone who speaks and acts with some kind of authority. But we live in egalitarian times, which is why the men are taught that to consider looks (or to talk about it with others as if they are considering looks) is the same thing as being a pig. And the women are taught that to look for a high status male who can lead others is to be a frothy little bit of nothing.

And yet the way of the world continues. Men start with how women look, and women start with how men act. Acknowledging these realities has fallen into disfavor, and so people avoid acknowledging them (even to themselves) *but they continue to act on the basis of them.*

Now every sensible Christian should know that the basics of attraction are merely what gets the second look, what garners the thoughtful consideration. And at this level, men are attracted by looks—hair, figure, face, liveliness. This is entry level for them, and so a man who stays there is a fool. Charm is deceitful, etc. (Prov. 31:30).

But we are not talking about what attracts them—the subject for another letter. I am talking about what attracts you. There is a masculine counterpart to the "charm is deceitful" principle. Machismo is deceitful also, and so you should be cautious. But you also need to not feel bad that you give a guy a second look because of it.

Just as charm is *not* deceitful if a woman has a gentle and quiet spirit (1 Pet. 3:4), because the charm goes all the way down, so also masculinity is not machismo—provided it goes all the way down.

So then, on to your list. I am going to provide a sample list below, with some commentary. This is only a sample list—as will become apparent, parts of it need to be on your list, while other parts of it are just placeholders, according to your tastes. The main thing is to note the structure of the list—need to have, good to have, would like to have, that kind of thing.

NEED TO HAVE

He must be a God-fearing man, attending worship faithfully, a conscientious Bible reader, one who consistently walks with God.

You do not want to be married to anyone who does not honor God as God. If he does not honor God, then it is because he in some way wants to be his own god, and you don't want to be married to anyone who wants to be a god.

He must be someone who naturally and readily commands your respect.

One of the central things the New Testament requires of wives is that they honor and respect their husbands. You do not want this to be a steep uphill climb. Do you naturally look up to him? And related to this, see the point below about attraction.

He must be committed to Christian education for any children you will have.

One of the central things you will do together with your husband is the rearing of your children. You do not want to be at cross-purposes with your husband when it comes to how you are going to do this.

He must be attractive to you.

This one admits of misunderstanding, but it is still important. I touched on this above, and will develop it some below. I am *not* talking someone who causes schoolgirl flutters, but rather someone you look up to and respect. This is because respect is an erotic necessity, and for many women it is an unrecognized erotic necessity. This aspect of the relations between men and women has been slandered horribly, as though conservative Christians are all about the domineering male, but the fact remains. C.S. Lewis points this out in *That Hideous Strength*.

"I see," said the Director. "It is not your fault. They never warned you. No one has ever told you that obedience—humility—is an erotic necessity. You are putting equality just where it ought not to be."[1]

And in a essay entitled "Equality," C.S. Lewis also says this:

This is the tragi-comedy of the modern woman; taught by Freud to consider the act of love the most important thing in life, and then inhibited by feminism from that internal surrender which alone can make it a complete emotional success. Merely for the sake of her own erotic pleasure, to go no further, some degree of obedience and humility seems to be (normally) necessary on the woman's part.[2]

So he must be attractive to you, but you must also have a good understanding of the laws of attraction. If you are not attracted to a guy because he is a milksop, you shouldn't feel bad about that. You are pleasing God through not being attracted. You are doing your duty. But if there is a guy you actually do respect, but you are not crushing on him, or your heart is not doing a gymnastic floor exercise, and as a result you worry that you are not "attracted," this means you that probably are misinterpreting the

1. *That Hideous Strength* (1996; New York: Scribner, 1945), 146.
2. *Present Concerns* (Orlando, FL: Harcourt, 1986), 19.

laws of attraction at the deeper level. You are not attracted to a guy you know you could lead around. Good for you. But you might *think* you are not attracted to a guy because you are nervous about where he might lead you. Not so good.

GOOD TO HAVE

He must be a man who reads.

You grew up in a family of books. This is the kind of thing I know you value, and it would be a trial to your soul if married to a man uninterested in books.

He should be the kind of man who will probably wind up in church leadership some day.

This is under "good to have" instead of "need to have" because there are plenty of godly Christian men who have no need to become elders or deacons. He might be too busy feeding you and the ten kids. But it is fine to put a pin in it and fine to have on your list.

NICE TO HAVE

These are the sorts of things you should have on your list, but be willing to adjust as the situation unfolds. This is because you might think you would be blessed by something in parallel, when you would actually be blessed by a contrast. Sit loose with this kind of thing.

He should be a man who likes living in the Pacific Northwest.

You would like to stay relatively close to your extended family.

He should be decent when it comes to playing lawn darts.

Your family always has lawn darts tournaments at your family reunions, and you don't want to be embarrassed.

Our respective families should be similar when it comes to cultural issues.

You don't want your kids suffering whiplash on alternative Thanksgivings.

SPECIAL CATEGORY/PRAYER REQUEST/LUCK OF THE DRAW

He should be aggressive enough, and well-endowed enough, to satisfy you sexually.

Because you and he are both Christians, this is not something you can ascertain directly. You are not supposed to ascertain it directly. The world thinks nothing of living together as sort of a test drive, thinking this provides "beforehand

knowledge," but it actually doesn't. Couples who refrain from sex before marriage, and who are faithful
to one another in marriage, are as a general rule far
more satisfied sexually than those who fancy themselves "experienced." Experience in fornication is
not experience in marital happiness.

I used the phrase "luck of the draw" above, but
that is only a matter of appearances. It is not really a matter of luck. Although you are not to come
together sexually until the honeymoon, this is still
something you should think about, and have some
awareness of. Having said this, you can draw reasonable inferences from certain proxy considerations.

When two rams on the side of a mountain are in
an epic head butting battle, what are they doing?
They are in a battle having to do with access to the
female. I speak in a parable, but a quarterback and a
linebacker are doing the same thing. Now some are
offended by this kind of thinking, but they should
grow up and deal with it.

One of the things we have done to muddle ourselves is to pretend that certain aspects of our lives
are not sexual in nature when they are entirely sexual in nature. But we have cordoned them off into
a separate mental category, and then are offended
when someone recognizes the sexual connection
anyhow.

Or perhaps we sometimes recognize the sexual connection when whatever it is gets to extreme
levels. What is the point of high heels? The point of

high heels is to accentuate the buttocks, and this is something we might admit if confronted with a trophy wife in ankle-busters and a silver lame dress. And there are ways of putting on makeup that are supposed to signal a mock arousal. But don't get me wrong. There are modest ways of putting on make-up, and there are modest heels out there. But there are no asexual heels.

In a similar way, there is no asexual football game. A man's sexual interest and ability to pursue you is directly related to testosterone. As a chaste Christian woman, you are to have no direct knowledge of how that would translate into the bedroom. But here is the good news. Testosterone does other stuff, which means that you can have that knowledge indirectly. But you can only have that knowledge if you are not kidding yourself about what is going on. We are sexual beings. We were created as sexual beings, and we are supposed to take it into account. But we are also rational beings, which means that we should do so intelligently. See what I wrote earlier about the laws of attraction.

So here now, I am going to draw this to a close. I see that your uncle is embarrassing you.

Your uncle,
Douglas

NINE

THE ART OF ATTRACTION

Dear Darla,

I alluded to this in my last letter, and I think it is time to address the art of attracting. We have covered what might attract you to him, and so now we should spend a little time on what might attract him to you. Some of what I am going to address here is no doubt old news to you. You have been brought up well, and are a diligent and modest Christian girl, and after I have discounted for all avuncular pride, you are quite a pretty girl, with no need of work in that department.

But we still have to talk about it. We live in a time when egalitarianism has reached near manic levels, which means you will no doubt have to defend certain common sense truths that your great grandmother never had to defend at all. There was a time when common sense was more common than it is now.

So let's begin with the modesty issue. And the starting point here has to be with the right of Christian teachers, particularly Bible teachers who are male, to speak to the issue. You really haven't seen incandescent fury until you have read a comments thread of women responding to the exhortation from some online brother, in which he expressed the sentiment that there ought to be less skin/less sin around here.

To dispense with that issue somewhat abruptly, the prophet Isaiah was male (Isa. 3:16ff), the apostle Peter was male (1 Pet. 3:3), and the apostle Paul was male (1 Tim. 2:9). And they all address feminine decorum.

When it comes to modesty, there are two things that Scripture forbids. The first is flamboyance, and the second is sexual impropriety. With regard to the first, you shouldn't be decked out like a circus pony. This is the emphasis we see in the passages I cited earlier. But you should know there is no apostolic injunction against a cute ponytail held in place with a red rubber band. They were talking about ornate architectural achievements piled up on a woman's head, with gold dust sprinkled over it. They were talking about hair that would have been admired by fools at Versailles, during a particularly decadent party. Not only should you not try to do anything like that, neither should you *lean* in that direction.

With regard to the second aspect of it, you should avoid anything that makes you look sexually available, sexually easy, or sexually cheap. When the young idiot in Proverbs is seduced, this was achieved in part by the fact that his feminine destruction was *dressed* "like a harlot" (Prov. 7:10). This again is common sense. If you are not that kind of girl, then you shouldn't advertise like you were that kind of girl. If you weren't going to sell the car, then why did you put the ad in the paper?

Having said all this, it has been too easy for prim Christians to veer off into a plain Jane Christianity, as though the Spirit was summoning us to explore the deeper attractions of Gnosticism. In the passage mentioned earlier, Peter is not telling Christian women to reject ornament. Rather, his point was to encourage the inner beauty of a gentle and quiet spirit, of great worth in God's sight, and the source of lasting beauty. So that was *how* the holy women of old used to adorn themselves for their husbands, who had eyes in their heads.

A woman's physical attractiveness is not an irrelevant attribute. It is not the case that only superficial observers take notice of such things. We know this because the scriptural writers were not superficial observers, obviously, and they comment on it. Abigail, we are told, was both beautiful and intelligent (1 Sam. 25:3). Sarai was a beautiful woman (Gen. 12:11). Rebekah was an attractive woman also (Gen. 26:7). The author of Genesis records the fact that Rachel had a beautiful face and a really nice body (Gen. 29:17). The patriarchs knew what they were about. The Shulamite was dark, but comely (Song of Sol. 1:5). The Israelites were given a law for those occasions when they noticed a beautiful woman among the captives (Deut. 21:11). In short, feminine beauty is a thing, and the biblical writers comment on it frequently.

The only reason modern Christians want to flatten all of this is because they have been influenced by a feminist egalitarianism, and they want to act like it is a scriptural holiness. It is not. It is unholiness. The end of that twisted road is plus-sized Victoria Secret models, offered to a bemused public in the hope that we will all agree to go along with their delusions.

As one astute observer noted, when an attractive but scantily clad woman shows up online, the denunciations are that the image is demeaning and oppressive. When an obese and scantily clad woman shows up online, it is somehow stunning and brave. Now biblical Christians disapprove of displaying either woman in this way, the first because it is immodest, the second because it is immodest and demented.

So given the fact that you are an attractive Christian girl who would like to get married, what should you do in this department?

There is a natural temptation to think that your attractiveness is at its peak while you are in your twenties. This is not a temptation because it is false; it is a temptation because of the *truth* in it. Scripture tells us that charm is deceitful and beauty is vain, but that a woman who fears the Lord is to be praised (Prov. 31:30). But charm can be deceitful in at least two ways. One of them the guys have to watch out for, but the other trap is something *you* need to watch out for.

Charm is deceitful when it seems to say to a man that a harridan is as charming inside as she is outside. But Christian men are told to look for a beauty that starts all the way on the inside and that works it's way *out*. Nobody wants to marry a whited sepulcher. Charm is not deceitful when it goes all the way through. Charm is deceitful to men when it is superficial, on the surface only.

But charm can deceive a woman also. She can assume that if she has the goods, she will continue to have them for at least a couple of decades. But this is radically false. And if she combines this erroneous assumption with the feminist propaganda, which the world serves up to us non-stop, that she should postpone marriage and children so that she can concentrate on her career, she is quite likely painting herself into a bad corner. It is a sad affliction when women find themselves in this position through no fault of their own. But this sadness is compounded when they find themselves in this position because of poor choices they made under the influence of feminist lies. You *can't* have it all, so in this regard you should trust God and think like an insurance company. Your chances of marrying well are much higher when you are in your early twenties. You should feel absolutely free to say *no* to a guy for sound reasons. You should not say *no* to a good man for foolish or nebulous reasons.

So then, cultivate inner beauty. Walk with God. Read your Bible. Confess your sins. Second, do this in places where men are around. Don't play hide and seek. Third, don't you be chasing them. Fourth, cultivate your domesticity. Learn to cook, for example. And last, dress with self-respect. Do your hair and makeup the same way. Do all this as though God is watching, because He is.

Your uncle,
Douglas

TEN

TRANSACTIONS AND COVENANTS

Dear Darla,

One of the hurdles that modern young women have to get over with regard to their thinking about marriage is the apparent transactional appearance of it. There is that surface appearance to begin with, and the plausibility of the charges leveled against it by the feminists have seeped into the backs of more than a few minds. That charge is that the "patriarchy" is simply a highly organized prostitution ring.

Now the first part of this letter is not going to seem like "relationship advice" at all, but I trust that by the end it should come into focus a bit more.

Back in the day, as it is thought, the village chief would buy a bride for his son, and the bride price was three chickens and a cow. The facile assumption is then made that a dowry is simply the financial price that must be paid in order for the chief's son to have access to sex. And how is that not prostitution?

I trust you see that the subject is a complicated one, and I trust that you also feel that it can be emotionally charged. Time-honored customs, such as the father of the bride walking his daughter down the aisle and "giving" her away, are thought by more traditional Christians to be sweet and all, and everybody in our circles still does it. But how do we answer the hard feminist challenge that there was no "giving" at all? There was a *fee*. Marriage is just decorated prostitution.

But let me be careful. I don't want to rub all your fur the wrong way all at once, and so let me outline the Christian resolution of this dilemma right at the front—which is the idea of *covenant*. I will then try to clear up some obvious questions after the fact.

Prostitution is obviously a major moral problem, but it is not a moral problem because it *includes* a financial/sexual transaction. It is a problem because of everything that it *leaves out*. Prostitution is a truncated parody of the marriage covenant, not a complete alternative to marriage. When a man is joined to his wife, the two become one flesh (Gen. 2:24; Matt. 19:5), and when a man is joined to a prostitute, the two become one flesh (1 Cor. 6:16). It it not some "other" thing, but rather a stripped down caricature.

Now a covenant is a solemn bond, sovereignly administered, with attendant blessings and curses. When it is a marriage covenant, it is a solemn bond that encompasses all of our natural life, all our natural children, all our natural goods, and so on. It does not cover a certain portion of our lives; the marriage state encompasses everything. There is no part of a married man's life in which he can be "unmarried." It involves all that he is and does.

A man's encounter with a prostitute strips away a lifetime of provision, and reduces it to a one-time cash payment, and in exchange, she renders him sex. The travesty here is everything that is *missing*. The feminist critique wants to say that the problem is the presence of sex for money. The real problem is that it is not nearly enough sex for not nearly enough money. And when those things get to the levels where they need to be, then many other aspects of life are swept up in all the excitement—car seats, minivans, mortgage payments, commuting to work, family vacations, white picket fences, dinner conversations, the works.

So Scripture is very clear that marriage is a covenant. The loose woman forgets the *covenant* of her God (Prov. 2:17). The men who are chided by Malachi for their marital treachery are told that they have been false to their wives by *covenant* (Mal. 2:14).

Now again, a covenant is a solemn bond, sovereignly administered, with attendant blessings and curses. And the marriage covenant is an all-encompassing covenant. With that said, you have to remember that not all transactions are covenants, but that all covenants are transactions. This means that when you go to the gardening store and buy a little hand shovel, that is a commercial transaction—but it does not rise to the level of a covenant. When a man and a woman stand up in front of a church and exchange vows, a transaction is happening there as well. But it is not *merely* a financial transaction. It is much, much bigger than that.

At this point, let me make a few more points about the scriptural grounding for all of this, and then I can finish by talking about how it is important for you to understand—living here in the twenty-first century as you do. I can finish by trying to make it relevant to you.

When Boaz redeemed Ruth, he was buying the land, and she was entailed with the land. Naomi was selling a parcel of land that had belonged to her late husband (Ruth 4:3). Boaz offered it to the unnamed relative, who said he would redeem the land (which was a financial transaction). Boaz then told him that Ruth came with the deal—he would have to buy her too (Ruth 4:5). At this the kinsman balked because he did not want to endanger the name of his line, and because he wanted to preserve his name, his name faded into oblivion. Boaz told the elders in the gate that he had *purchased* Ruth (Ruth 4:10). So Boaz purchased the land, and Ruth also, and she became his free wife (Ruth 4:13). She was not his concubine (a slave wife), but rather a free woman in Israel. And this is because the presence of a financial commitment as one of the terms of the covenant does not result in chattel slavery. A bride price or dowry does *not* mean that a woman is being purchased like an object off the shelf.

A biblical dowry was (in effect) divorce insurance. A suitor who paid the dowry was endowing his wife with a fund that stayed in her name. If he later divorced her for no cause, or for burning the toast, she kept that money. If he was going to be an unreasonable man, then he was going to pay a price for being an unreasonable man. Her father could also add to her endowment, which an unreasonable man would also forfeit. That endowment was hers.

If she was guilty of adultery, however, the case was different. He didn't lose anything if she played him false. This standard is likely what lies behind the puzzling divorce law in Deuteronomy 24:1-4. Husband #1 divorces his wife for *cause* (meaning that she forfeits the dowry). Husband #2 divorces her (not for cause), meaning that she still has her dowry, or he dies, meaning that she has the inheritance. Under those circumstances, husband #1 is prohibited from financially profiting by maintaining two opposite positions—i.e. that she was somehow worthy of divorce for cause and also somehow worthy to marry again.

So this might seem like the long way around, but here is why it matters to you, and how it should affect your thinking. The marriage covenant involves all of our stuff. The biblical view of marriage is a community property kind of thing. Because of the covenant, the one flesh union becomes a sacred identity. In the absence of covenant, as happens with prostitution, the one flesh union becomes a travesty. But it is not the presence of sex and money that makes it that travesty, but rather the absence of the covenant. This is because the covenant encompasses all of life, and speaks the truth about all of that life.

The relationship between a man and a woman, bound by holy matrimony, is not just a matter of their hearts being entwined. Rather, everything is entwined. And because everything is entwined, there must be standards, sanctions, terms, conditions. A covenant has all of those things. So lease agreements, contracts, car rental forms, and marriages do all have certain areas of overlap. But the marriage covenant is the king of them all. When it comes to earthly transactions, none is greater or more profound than marriage.

Say a couple of businessmen strike a deal. In six months, one of them will deliver 100 widgets by a certain specified date, and the other guy will pay $1000 dollars for them. A couple months later, the two men happen to meet at some social event. In the course of their conversation, they discover that the one guy's widget factory had burned down, such that he can't make them, and the other guy's customer, who was going to market the widgets for him, had canceled his order. Now, in this circumstance, do the two men have the authority to shake hands and call the whole deal off? Yes, because it is their deal. It was *their* contract. They made it, they can tear it up. They are lords of their own contract. They can do this because it is a lesser contract.

Now suppose you have a married couple, married for three years, and in the course of a conversation one evening they both discover that both of them want out of the marriage. Neither one loves the other one. No kids, no joint property. Divorce would be pretty simple. Do they get to shake hands and call it off? No, they do not. They do not get to do this because they are not the ones who joined together. This is a covenant, not a contract. What *God* has joined together, let no man separate (Mark 10:9).

Now comes the practical part.

When romantic or sentimental young girls think that marriage is simply about being soul mates, or best friends, or anything like that, they are leaving out most of life. Not only so, but they are seeking to have some nebulous feeling of love be the bonding agent. And then, when that feeling is gone, or has shifted into a form that they don't recognize, they feel like the marriage is dead.

The covenant is like a concrete foundation—gray, cold, hard, straight lines everywhere. This is simply the way it is—if you want your house to remain standing. When the concrete trucks drive away, the covenant has been poured. Because the foundation is straight, you can put up all the cushions and curtains of sentiment and emotional attachment that you want to. What you cannot do is heap up cushions, curtains, rugs, pillows, and afghans as a foundation, and try to build a straight stud wall on that pile. It won't work, as modern divorce rates show.

And so the central question for you, in considering your prospects, is this one. Is he a good man? Will he love me as Christ loved the church? Will he keep covenant?

Your uncle,
Douglas

ELEVEN

COMPARED TO WHAT?

Dear Darla,

Now there are some strategic and tactical implications of what I wrote in my last few letters. It is time for us to game some of this out. Let's get practical— or a bit more practical in your *thinking*, at any rate.

You are in your mid-twenties now, and so you may have noticed that requests to go out with guys are starting to taper off. If you haven't noticed that yet, and if you don't get married in the next few years, you can be assured that at some point you will notice it. Forty-two-year-old women don't get the same attention that twenty-two-year-old women do. And complaining about things like this is a fool's game; it is like complaining about gravity. Wise women work with the way the world actually is, and not the way they would have liked it to have been.

Now I do need to emphasize something at the front end of all this. I have no desire whatever to be involved in pressuring any girl to say *yes* to some guy that she doesn't want to say *yes* to. Nobody needs authority figures (parents, pastors, or even uncles) to be leaning heavily on young ladies under their charge just because the authority figure went to college back in the day with Murgatroyd B. Schwartz's parents, and that is why they would like her to give him a second look. Look. The world has enough sorrow in it.

However, there are different kinds of sorrow in the world. There is the sorrow of unhappy marriages, whether caused by sin or by a marital mismatching of gifts and personalities, on the one hand, but on the other, there is also the sorrow of loneliness. I have written elsewhere on the fact that undesired singleness is an affliction, not a gift, and so that must be taken into account as well. That possible sorrow needs to be one of the variables in the calculation.

And so this is how to frame the question to yourself. Now during the era when the guys are still clustering around, it is natural (and right) for you to want to sort through them. There is no way to say *no* to some and *yes* to another without comparisons.

You don't want to inject snark into your comparisons—because no guy ought ever to be snarked at just because he paid you a compliment—but at the same time, if you say *no* to Bill and *yes* to John, the unavoidable conclusion is that you thought that John was "better" for you. He offered more of what you were looking for, and Bill did not. Don't chafe at this—this is how God decided to govern the world. Bill shouldn't chafe at it either.

But here is something that you need to seriously consider. It needs to be one of your thought experiments. You preferred John to Bill, and you had every right to do so. But now change the comparison. What about Bill over against nobody? If you are forty and unmarried, is *that* situation to be preferred to being the wife of Bill? It is not just Bill vs. John. It is also Bill vs. ten years from now having yet another a glass of wine on your deck in the evening by yourself.

I do not bring this up in order to worry you, terrify you, or panic you. This loneliness prospect is one that some young women think about far too much, while others don't consider it much at all. Those who think about it too much will face the temptation to give into what we call "settling." This conjures up visions of Charlotte settling for Mr. Collins, and you imagine yourself in *that* position, which is why you then wake up from your nightmare, gasping for air and in a bad flop sweat. Yeah, so don't settle. Don't do that.

Because settling is bad. But you have known me for long enough that perhaps you might anticipate my next question. *By what standard?* If Elizabeth had asked herself, ten years after the Mr. Darcy thing didn't work out, if she had done right by spurning Mr. Collins, her answer would be just as decisive then as it was the day she first shut him down. She wouldn't have second thoughts about it. You should prefer loneliness to some matches.

But there are many young women who say no to a real live Bill because they expect that there will be a John who shows up any week now. However, at the moment, John is still imaginary, and for many girls, that's the way he stays. So what is it that keeps this ethereal John (who stands her up for *every* date) in the running?

And this is where I might get to meddling a little bit. There is a modern doctrine going about that tells young people that they should hold out for "the one," and that they will know "that one" when he arrives, and they will know it "in their heart." Or perhaps, if they were catechized by Cher by means of "The Shoop Shoop Song," it needs to be found "in his kiss." The road to many a broken heart was paved with wisdom like that, right there.

But this is the dogmatic foundation of the entire chick flick industry, and a lot of damage has been done by it. "The one" looks into your eyes and discovers the depths of the real you. "The one" is your best friend forever. "The one" is a true soul mate, appointed as such by your guardian angel, or perhaps by Gabriel. "The one" takes you as you are without ever requiring you to take him as he is. And therein lies a tale.

A whole lot of this is just pornography for the emotions. And, while I am sorry to be rude, take a moment to compare how similar it is to sexual porn. Actual women complain that guys are idiots to be attracted to the women of porn, who are just airbrushed cartoons. They say, with a justified grievance, that "real women" aren't like that. How could anybody be lured away from real relationship by some two-dimensional twinkie? Well, the answer is simple—it happens the same way that women are lured away from real relationship with an actual *guy* by the contrivances of some smooth-talking scriptwriter.

When you realize you want to spend the rest of your life with somebody, you want the rest of your life to start as soon as possible.

Well, it was a million tiny little things that, when you added them all up, they meant we were supposed to be together . . . and I knew it. I knew it the very first time I touched her. It was like coming home . . . only to no home I'd ever known . . . I was just taking her hand to help her out of a car and I knew. It was like . . . magic.

When I saw your eyes that first time, I realized that looking into them was the only possible way I could ever see into my own.

Out of those three quotes, I made up only one of them.[1] If you ever meet a guy who talks like that, please take the advice of your uncle and *run*.

At that part of the movie, all the guys mutter *sheesh* to themselves, but do not say anything. They do not say anything because this is currently an approved lie. They mutter this the same way that the women say *sheesh* at the nudity of the movies. What this double standard means is that men must not be lied to in the same way that women can be lied to. But the real standard is that no one ought to be lied to.

The problem is that what women often mean by "real relationship" is just as artificial and contrived as the porn is. Imagined conversations that are dark roast coffee for the morning, with a sensitive swirl of gentle cream on the black surface, or settle down like dying embers at the end of a pleasant evening's fire, are conversations that do not reflect how the mundane flow of regular life usually goes. *Those* conversations more frequently have to do with mashed potatoes, how work was today, and who's picking up the kids?

1. The first is from the movie *When Harry Met Sally*, and the second is from the movie *Sleepless in Seattle*.

This is not meant to slam an appropriate poetic element in our lives, or a romantic sexual element either. That kind of thing really is part of real life. The thing I am targeting is unrealistic expectations, and when someone has unrealistic expectations, they generally get applied to *all* of life. More specifically, on the point we are discussing, they are applied to prospective suitors, and the young woman wonders if he could live up to the levels she has been imagining for herself. And if he is a typical young man of godly character, the answer to that is "almost certainly not." But what that should reveal is the inadequacy of artificially constructed expectations.

When I ask *"By what standard?,"* the implied answer to my rhetorical question is always to be Scripture. A young woman should always be asking if a particular young man has the capacity of character to be a biblical husband to her. Those last two words, *to her,* do bring in a subjective element. Can his pickup truck pull her trailer? If she respects him, and if others in her life also respect him, and she knows the value of their respect, that is something to take seriously.

Provided they are biblical standards, it is essential to have high standards. Don't settle for "a little" dishonest, or "a little" lazy, or "a little" bit of coasting in his reading of the Word. *Don't settle.* But notice that these are all character issues, and scriptural standards. Whether he is "dreamy," or as outgoing as your brother, or prepared to accept you as you are, are not in the same category.

And since I have mentioned it again, let me say just one thing about this "accepting you as you are" virtue. Why is it a virtue for men to accept their women as they are, but not for women to do the same? If it were truly a good thing, as all women appear to appreciate, then why don't more women accept men as they are? Because that would be a bad idea, that's why. Bad idea both directions.

Your uncle,
Douglas

TWELVE

THE RIGHT KIND OF BEAUTY TREATMENT

Dear Darla,

Whenever we feel stuck in some place, the temptation is to think that we know and understand all the variables. We know *that* we are stuck, and we therefore assume we know *why* we are stuck.

You notice your birthdays are continuing to go by, and you had assumed when you were a little girl that you would be married by this point, but you aren't, and so what's the deal?

But when you ask yourself, *"What's the deal?,"* the temptation is to think you necessarily see the full problem accurately. You don't have the solution, but you think the nature of the problem is self-evident. The problem is that there are not enough guys, or the guys are not coming around because somebody needs to light a fire under them, or that you need to change what you are doing with your hair, and so on. And I do grant that those things that you see could easily be *part* of the problem.

You see the basic fact of the problem, and you likely have identified some of the factors that have created it.

But one of the things you should also want to do is run a spiritual inventory in your soul, in order to see whether there are any internal and invisible things that are getting in the way. Sometimes these internal things are hang-ups that you half-way know about, but don't like thinking about, and other times you don't know anything whatever about them, or you know about them but reckon them as being among your virtues. The question is how can you get at those things which you cannot see? Or better, how might you dislodge them so that you could see them?

With that said by way of tantalizing introduction, let me go straight to my suggestion, and then follow it up with some comments on how it might be related to you in your unmarried state.

My suggestion is that you should sit down and write your father what Nancy and I call a "respect letter." We have seen this have a big impact in the lives of many young women. We also know that you have a good relationship with your dad, and so you are not trying to fix anything in your relationship, but that doesn't mean that it won't dislodge some things in your heart when you sit down to write it. And if you pick those things up and look at them closely, you might learn some things about your relationship to your future husband.

You don't have a husband to relate to, and so what I am urging you to do is to practice on your dad. When you go through this process of respecting your dad, it gets at a number of things in a young woman's soul. It is also going to do a different kind of number on your dad, but it will not be negative at all. He will really appreciate it.

Let me flip this around so you can see more readily what I mean. Suppose you overheard me giving this same kind of counsel to Dawson. Before he had a girl, suppose I told him to practice on his mom. Giving attention, being thoughtful, sending flowers on appropriate occasions. If he set about doing that, you would think it wonderful, and sweet, and thoughtful.

But you will have noticed that I told him to write a different kind of letter than I am telling you to write. He should write a love letter to his mom, and you should write a respect letter to your dad. This is because men and women are different, and the scriptural emphasis on their assigned duties is correspondingly different.

Scripture tells husbands to love their wives, and Scripture tells wives to respect their husbands. Whenever I get into this, I always want to qualify it, because Scripture also teaches all Christians, regardless of their sex, to love their neighbor (Matt. 22:39), and it also tells all Christians, regardless of their sex, to respect their neighbor (1 Pet. 2:17).

But when the Bible is addressing men as men, and women as women, it tells the men to love, and it tells the women to respect. This tells us at least two things. First, it tells us what the other sex needs to be receiving from us. From the Lord's command to Peter to "feed my sheep," we may infer that the sheep need food. Women *need* love, and men *need* respect.

The second thing we can infer is that shepherds need to be reminded of their duties with regard to this feeding. Men need to be *reminded* that they must love, and women need to be *reminded* that they must respect. It is easy to drift into a state where we take life for granted, along with all the other people in our lives. And when we learn that we need to be reminded of a particular duty, we should assume that we have a propensity to drift away from that duty.

If I told Dawson to practice his love and affirmation on his mom, and he found the words sticking in his throat, and he was overcome with a strange and unidentified reluctance, he should conclude that something was going wrong. His "love muscles" were atrophying. The same thing is true of you—your "respect muscles" were atrophying. The reminders came just in time.

When you sit down to write this respect letter, you should focus on his *abilities* and *achievements*. This is a different coinage system than women tend to use with one another, but it is what you should focus on. Or, to change the metaphor, men run on diesel and women run on regular. Do not put the wrong fuel in the wrong tank. Tell him how much you respect—and use that word *respect*—how hard he works. Tell him how smart he is. Tell him how you appreciate his military service. Tell him how much you admire his strength. You get the picture. Now, despite the fact that you already have a great relationship with your dad, he is going to appreciate this letter very much.

Now, on to what it might dislodge in you. Despite the fact that you have a good relationship with your dad, and despite the fact that you grew up in conservative Christian circles, and despite the fact that you are regular Bible reader, the chances are excellent to outstanding that you have been influenced by our surrounding feminist culture more than you thought you were. What this does is provide an excellent purging opportunity.

And also, I should mention in passing that this will help you sympathize with those friends of yours who have no dad, or a lousy relationship with their dad. They have a much greater challenge than do you—but it is a challenge you all must face. If you have friends in that category, it is doubly important that they write the same kind of letter. No lies, no flattery, but rather simple respect. What *can* you respect about him?

So what do I mean "purging opportunity"? You may notice a strange reluctance creeping in. If something about this doesn't sit right, or the whole thing might stirs up vague and nebulous resentments toward men generally, or indignation toward the entitlement of the masculine, then the exercise of writing this letter is doing its work in you. They work it does in your dad is simple gratitude. Men need respect; they run on it. But what it awakens in you is a realization of the degree to which feminism has taught you to wince at certain things, and how much it makes you want to overreact, and how down deep it makes you want to misrepresent the duty to yourself so that you don't have to feel so bad about apparently being a closet feminist. "Oh, so am I supposed to run up to some guy, squeeze his bicep and say, 'My hero!'?"

The bottom line is this. When women appreciate men generally, as a class, and when women admire and respect displays of biblical masculinity and are not afraid to admire them *openly*, and they have these sentiments all the way down, this demeanor is profoundly attractive.

But what Christian women do, halfway trained by the feminists, is this—they say, "Oh, so I am supposed to act like some silly little schoolgirl, in love with the quarterback because he's so 'dreamy'?" In short, they misrepresent—because nothing in the world is easier to misrepresent, especially in this climate.

What this letter to your father will do is that it will help you become a strong and biblically minded Christian woman, one who loathes feminism and all its works. Understanding feminism, and learning how to hate it rightly, is, when it comes to influencing the right kind of Christian man, a very arduous course of beauty treatments.

Your uncle,
Douglas

THIRTEEN

NO ROM-COM ENDING

Dear Darla,

One of the things that is likely lurking in the back of your mind is the prospect or possibility of never getting married. I say "prospect," but perhaps a better word for it is anxiety or worry. The *what-ifs* start to crowd into your mind, and you don't know what to do with them quite.

Making matters worse, you also have some older friends at church who are still not married, and you cannot fathom why they are not married. They are lovely, accomplished, intelligent, and would make marvelous wives and mothers. You don't know what to say to them when they open up to you about it, and they probably don't realize the extent to which some of their distress gets internalized by you and gathered up into your emotional weather.

Obviously, you can't fix the problem by charging off and proposing to some guy, and so all you can do is sit there and lament the ways things are done. Why do the *girls* have to wait?

So you can't fix the problem of being unmarried, because that takes two. But you can fix the problem of how you are thinking about it—that only takes one. For a little background on all this, I have written on this general subject before.[1]

A big part of our problem in the church today is the prevalent teaching that singleness "is a gift." The difficulty here is that in the vast majority of cases, this is just not true. Because we believe in the sovereignty of God, we know that everything that happens to us in our lives occurs as the outworking of His decretal will. He determined *everything* that comes to pass, and He did this before the foundation of the world. God freely and unalterably ordains whatever comes to pass, as all good Calvinists affirm.

But what this apparently soft and encouraging sentiment is doing—I am referring to the teaching

1. "7 Reasons Young Men Should Marry Before Their 23rd Birthday," *Blog and Mablog*, April 11, 2016, https://dougwils. com/books-and-culture/s7-engaging-the-culture/7-reasons-young-men-marry-23rd-birthday.html.
"Singleness as Affliction," *Blog and Mablog*, November 25, 2020, https://dougwils.com/books-and-culture/s7-engaging-the-culture/singleness-as-affliction.html.

that singleness is a gift—is to actually adopt and implement the harshest expressions of the most hardshell Tishbite we might be able to find.

What would you say if you asked a friend to go with you to the hospital to comfort a friend who had just received a cancer diagnosis, and he said he would be happy to because in circumstances like this it is important to remind people that cancer is a gift? Is amputation a gift? Is bankruptcy a gift? Is the loss of a loved one a gift? In the sense that they all proceed from the decretal will of God, sure. But that is not how we usually handle the word gift.

The doctrine of God's foreordination of all things is an unspeakable comfort, and it particularly enables God's people to navigate hard providences. "This too has a purpose in God's larger plan, no matter how it hurts." That's good. But to argue that anything that comes from the hand of God must therefore be counted as a walk in the park, and you are an ingrate if you don't count it as a walk in the park, is a form of the most thoughtless, rude, insensitive, fatalistic, and hard-bitten Calvinism on the planet. And it goes without saying that it is not a biblical form of Calvinism either.

Getting your mind around this is truly liberating. It is difficult and hard to accept, but it is much easier to believe that God will strengthen and equip you to handle a most difficult circumstance than it will be to believe that God wants you to pretend that the loneliness isn't lonesome. With God's help you can climb a mountain. But you cannot—not even with God's help—pretend that mountain climbing is actually deep sea diving.

Telling the unmarried people in the church that their singleness is a gift and that they should be rejoicing in it is simply cruel. They should be rejoicing—because the Bible says to—but they are rejoicing in an affliction. And when you rejoice in an affliction, you are trusting God. You are not kidding yourself. When you think that your duty is to rename your bed of thorns, calling it a feather bed, and that you must do this because your pastor told you to, you are actually getting gas lit.

When the *what-ifs* crowd in, don't try to answer them. We don't know the future, and shouldn't pretend to know the future. What if I never get married? You should respond to this with something like, "If such is to be the case, Almighty Father, I give you thanks." You do this because we are commanded to—"Giving thanks always *for all things* unto God and the Father in the name of our Lord Jesus Christ" (Eph. 5:20). This is a command to thank God for all things, including hard things. It is not a command to pretend that hard things are soft things: "In every thing give thanks: for this is the will of God in Christ Jesus concerning you" (1 Thess. 5:18).

But if I could misapply a scriptural line from Hebrews, "we are confident of better things concerning you . . . though we speak in this manner"

(Heb. 6:9). I am in the highest degree confident that you are going to be married at some point, and I might even hint at having some insider information. If you are very polite in your next letter, I might even tell you more. I mean, the young men of today do have many problems, but they are not *blind.*

That said, you do have friends who may not be in that same position at all. They really might not get married, and no Rom-Com ending. What I have written is hard, true enough. But we can trust God with the hard, we can rest in Him when it is hard. But we cannot trust in Him if we are being delusional. These friends of yours should do a Bible study on the goodness of God's sovereignty, and trust in Him to help them deal with the world as it actually is.

A plain woman never marries. A beautiful woman marries three skunks in a row. A young wife gets cancer and dies. Another woman marries but is unable to have children. This is not said in the spirit of stoicism, but things are tough all over: "The heart knows its own bitterness, and no stranger shares its joy" (Prov. 14:10, ESV).

So as you rest in God's sovereign choices *now,* this makes it easier to trust in Him concerning all your tomorrows. He has planned good works for you to walk in (Eph. 2:10), and all of those good works are in the palm of His hand. Contentment now prepares you for contentment later. Obedience now prepares you for obedience later.

Enough for now.
Your uncle,
Douglas

FOURTEEN

THE ROSETTA STONE OF THE SEXES

Dear Darla,

I want to spend at least a little bit of time talking about the nature of the differences between men and women. This is important because we have something of an optical illusion going, and it runs in both directions.

If you were to travel to a foreign land, but one suitably exotic, you would be struck by all the differences, all the time, but struck in a certain way. You would be struck by *striking* differences, which would astonish, but they were striking differences that you *expected* to encounter, which is why you wouldn't be that astonished. You wouldn't be surprised because you expected to be surprised, and you were. But if you traveled to a country very much like our own, somewhere in the English speaking world, say, you would be constantly lured into thinking it was going to be the same, and then it wouldn't be. What did *that* traffic sign mean? Everything was going swimmingly, and then there was that little twist at the end.

It is like this between men and women. Living with a man is like visiting the UK for the first time, and for him, living with a woman is like going to New Zealand. The fact that men and women both speak English, and both live in the same town and drive on the same streets, and attend the same schools, gives them an awful lot in common. That is what lures you into complacency. But all of this information is being processed, by you and by him, on completely different operating systems.

Imagine that I, your dutiful uncle, have taken you aside, and I have said to you, "Darla, do you see those boys standing over there?" And you nod your head, indicating that you do. And so then I say, "That's a whole different country over there. They do things differently there." And someone else, my counterpart, could take any one of those boys aside, and say exactly the same thing about you and your girl friends.

There are two things that are really necessary for you to grasp in order to be able to deal with this. One is an absolute confidence in the authority of Scripture, and a belief that this authority speaks to the differences between men and women. This life between the sexes was God's idea, remember, and this means that He wants it this way. The second thing you need, and which I don't think I need to develop, is a sense of humor. If you really trust in God, and completely rely on His Word, you will get the joke.

Now in saying all this about God's design in the differences, we need to factor out things that are manifestly sinful—malice, anger, lust, hatred, and so on. Those are things that we Christians are at war with, men and women both, and which we must not in any way accommodate. In speaking about differences, I am not referring to toxic differences. But I am talking about things that are simply bewildering to you, and not things that God's Word flatly prohibits. All toxicity is different, but not all differences are toxic.

And so this is why you need to trust the Scriptures. Think of the Bible as a Rosetta Stone that will teach you how to interpret men, and not through a woman's lens. And men must not interpret women through a male lens. Men must receive their instruction about how to treat women from the one who *invented* women. Women must read the instruction manual also, and learn from the one who first designed men. And yes, men were apparently done on purpose. I say this because God understands men better than women do. God understands women better than men do, and He is the one who tells us all how to behave. As He does this, we can trust Him.

I will end all this with a practical example or two, but I want to hammer home the basic principle first. First, it is okay to be a man . . . but with qualifications. It is okay to be a man provided you were born a boy. It is okay to be a woman provided you were born a girl. We didn't used to have to go over things like this, but we do go over them these days.

It is also all right to be a man, but just not an arrogant man. A man is called to walk humbly with his God (Mic. 6:8). It is also all right to be a woman, provided you are a *humble* woman. And what this means is that you accept that you need guidance from God on what men and women are for, what their respective roles ought to be, and how they should treat one another. In short, it is necessary for men and women both to have a shared theology of the sexes. Neither sex has the capacity to originate such a theology (which would either be male imperium or female imperium), and so in order to share a theology of men and women, we all must receive it from outside this world. We must therefore be Bible readers, and straightforward Bible believers. This means that the patriarchy is what it is for us because of God the Father (Eph. 3:15), and not because Christianity was invented by males doing their thing.

So bring this down to earth. What I am saying here is that it is necessary to have these bedrock assumptions underneath my earlier letter on "understanding guys." That was simply a list of a number of the differences, along with practical advice on dealing them. This is what undergirds a proper understanding of those differences.

Suppose that a guy comes to town and asks out one of your friends. She declines. A couple weeks later he asks out another one of your friends. She goes out with him once or twice, but declines any further invitations. The third time he goes out with another girl who was very interested in him, but he doesn't ask her out again. Now, a couple of months in, suppose that he asks you out.

This is where you might feel affronted, as though he had violated some kind of scriptural standard, when he has done nothing of the kind. You might think that he is being callused or mercenary, or desperate, or on the hunt, or something, and you are more than a little peeved that he asked you out *fourth*. But he is just looking for a wife, which is a fine thing for him to do. You are looking for a husband too, but not *that* way. You don't like it being so obvious. But in that moment, you are thinking about it like a woman, not like a Christian.

Now granted, it could be possible for him to violate certain common protocols or manners surrounding this sort of thing. Suppose one of the girls who declined to go out with him again was immediately asked by him, "Well, do you think your roommate might be interested?" Okay, there *he* is thinking about it like an idiot, and not like a Christian. There is such a thing as acting foolishly in this area, as though any willing female will do. But take care that your reaction not be driven by a hidden doctrine of "the one," the doctrine that undergirds so many chick flicks. If a man needs an apartment, no one faults him for looking for an apartment. And if a man needs a wife, there is no sin in him looking for one. He should take care to mind his manners, but he doesn't need the women urging him to get off the dime, and then faulting him for continuing to try if two women turn him down.

And here is another example, and although it seems completely different than the first one, it is nevertheless shaped by the same foundational theology that I was writing about above. I want to take this illustration from congregational singing. We have worshiped at your church more than a few times, and one of the standout features of your worship is the singing. Your sanctuary has great acoustics, and your people really know how to sing. Moreover, on more than a few of your songs, the congregation knows how to break into parts, and there really is nothing like it.

One of the things I would encourage you to do, or to pray about doing, is this. In a fuguing tune, for example, when the basses start the refrain by themselves, and then the tenors join them, while you are waiting to sing your part, thank God for the men. You should be proud of the men being men. Thank God for the low voices, in other words, and listen to them with pride and appreciation. And ask God to help you with your kvelling. And the men should be thinking that they can't wait until the women join them, and the women should be glorying in the fact that the men are leading them.

This is a nice little exercise, where the men learn how to glory in their women, and the women learn how to glory in their men. You might be surprised at what hidden assumptions doing this might bring to the surface. And what you learn about yourself in such corporate interactions will transfer readily to an individual man when you eventually meet someone who is a genuine prospect.

All for now.

Your uncle,
Douglas

FIFTEEN

THE KILL SWITCH AND THE STEERING WHEEL

Dear Darla,

So in my last letter, I concluded with a reference to you meeting a genuine prospect, and I believe I even used the word "eventually." And now your mother has informed my wife that this may have happened. So . . . what's his name? My only concern here is that it not be Murgatroyd. *That* should be a deal breaker.

So, as you are already corresponding with your favorite uncle, I take it that you are not averse to a little avuncular advice. When you are all by yourself, unattached, "boys" as a topic is kind of out there in the abstract. And when you are married, Scripture sets down a very clear pattern for life between the sexes. But how are you supposed to behave when a guy has asked you out a few times? "What are the *rules*?"

There used to be shared cultural standards for dating and courtship, but those are largely gone now. This has been a function of the sexual revolution, the invention of the automobile, the sheer number of people in the country, the result of various subcultures jostling around, and different movements and fads within the church, which in their turn have led to different emphases that different families have. And so there you are, wondering what the expectations are. Don't worry. For you right now, they reduce to just a few principles.

I heard that this fine young gentleman has already called your dad, and has been given certain parameters by him. And I trust that your father has also talked to you about various challenges that I touched on in earlier letters—the need for guarding your heart, not daydreaming, and so on. That's all good, and if you want to, it might be helpful if you went back and reread those letters.

But here are some fresh observations for you, given the new circumstance you are in. I have one central thing for you this time, although I am sure there will be enough for a few more letters later.

This topic has to do with realizing that this young man you are going out with has no actual authority over you. He is taking you to a restaurant, and that does not make him your head. But at the same time, if the relationship gets a bit more serious, both you and he need to be mindful of the fact that he is "trying out" for the part of becoming your head. So how do you treat him in the interim? Before there is a covenant, you are the final authority over whether there is even going to be a relationship at all. After a covenant is made, he becomes the final authority in the relationship. And navigating that transition can be pretty tricky.

So supposing that you like his company, and that he likes yours, as indicated by the fact that he asked you out again, what are you to do? First, do *not* try to control the pace of the relationship. What I mean is this. Do not, on your seventh date, say anything like, "So, where *are* we in all this?" That's a perfectly reasonable question (at some point anyway), provided your dad asks it. So the issue is not whether you need that information (you might well need it), but rather the question is whether you are in charge of extracting it. You are not.

When a guy asks a girl out, whether it is for a first date, or for the twentieth date, she can say *yes*, or she can say *no*. That is fully her prerogative. What she shouldn't try to do is get control of the agenda, and then try to chair the meeting. But she *is* in charge of whether or not there is even going to be

a meeting. She determines that by saying *yes* or *no*.
But the fact that you have the kill switch does not
mean that you should have the steering wheel. And
many girls make that mistake. Let *him* have the
steering wheel, and if he needs help steering, in-
volve your dad. You should just sit in the passenger
seat, looking cute.

So once the meeting (i.e., the date) starts, she
shouldn't be asking him questions like, "What am
I? Your girlfriend? Your movie buddy? Your sister's
friend? Your future fiancé? Talk to me, Murgatroyd."

If she feels like he is dragging his feet—and lots
of guys do that—or is dithering somewhat—and
guys do that too—and she would like the relationship to get a little more forward momentum going,
then she should exercise this prerogative of hers
that I just mentioned. She should just say *no*.

It is up to her whether or not she gets into the car
on the passenger side. She doesn't have to go with
him. But if she goes with him, having gotten in on
the passenger side, she shouldn't try to steer.

Now if she says *no*, he of course is going to ask
why, and she should say, "Well, it is not my place
to tell you how to run your affairs." And he will say,
"But I really want to know. Did I say something
wrong? Are you mad at me?" And you should smile
and say of course you are not mad, but you don't
want to grab the steering wheel of anything, and
if he really wants to know more, he should talk to

your dad about it. And he will ask, "Are you break-ing up with me?"

Now this is the million-dollar question that you really wouldn't know how to answer. You don't know if you are breaking up as an item because you do not yet know if you even *are* an item. That is why you felt enormous internal pressure, over that cof-fee, to say, "Hey. Are we an item?" That is you taking the initiative, you taking the lead, you taking the position of the head. Don't do it.

If he asks you to go with him, and you want to, then go with him. If he asks you to go, and you don't want to, then don't go. But . . . and here is where the rub comes in . . . what if he is the kind of guy that you *would* like to go out with if only you had *some* idea of where you were going? If a girl is attracted to a guy, and he is showing some interest, she *hates* ambiguity. She hops in the car, but without know-ing if it is going to be Italian at some restaurant and back home again, or a cross-country road trip with forever at the end of it.

A long series of aimless, non-teleological hang out sessions is fun and all, but it gets old quick. But guys like the companionship of a pretty girl, and they can get comfortable with an undefined rela-tionship more readily than a girl can. If that starts to happen, he is content and she is exasperated. So in this I am not telling you how to break up with him—I am telling you how best to avoid the kind of exasperation that might result in you breaking up with him when you didn't really want to.

So if, under these circumstances, he does call your dad, you might want to know what your dad should say. That should be simple and straightforward. "Darla is reluctant to go out with anyone aimlessly. She likes you very well, but thinks that just hanging out doesn't have enough direction to it."

Now of course, your father may already have anticipated this problem and headed it off. He may have told Buster that he was free to take you out five times or so, and then after that they would need to have a talk about where this was going. That is probably the best approach, at least for my money. But if he didn't do that, you can just hand it right back to your dad anyhow. He won't mind. And five dates seems about right.

Your father is in a position to talk to him about the pace and direction of the relationship without you looking like *you* are "seizing the reins." When doing something like this, you really are wielding authority, but you are doing it in a feminine way.

Say that a woman had three suitors, and they all wanted to marry her. She is deciding between them, but in doing this she is deciding who is going to be her head and her authority—but *she* is the one making the decision.

The wife is bound by the law as long as her husband liveth; but if her husband be dead, *she is at liberty to be married to whom she will;* only in the Lord. (1 Cor. 7:39, emphasis added)

If this woman referred to in 1 Corinthians marries a particular man, then she would be called, by the standards of Scripture, to be submissive and obedient to that man. But *she* is the one who makes the selection. The metaphor might be off-putting to some, in these our feminist times, but a marriage is a little kingdom and the husband is a little king. Once married, he is the king of that little kingdom, and his decisions have real authority. But the woman has true authority also. She is in charge of the line of succession, and she is in charge of the coronation. If a man proposes to a woman, and she turns him down flat, it is her authoritative decision that results in him being "not a king."

The challenge for you will be to wield that kind of authority, in the right place, and in the right way, without becoming the kind of woman who mistakenly believes that this makes her the king. No. But if you select the right kind of man, you will be the queen, which is what you were made for.

Your uncle,
Douglas

SIXTEEN

LOVE, HONOR, AND OBEY

Dear Darla,

So his name is Trent, is it? Lucky dog.

This means that you are now going to be thinking through a number of the things I have written in the earlier letters, but now doing so in a very concrete way. Before it could all seem sort of abstract and out there . . . kind of ethereal. Now a very particular individual has shown up on your doorstep and wants to go out with you, and you are interested in doing so. How should you process this?

Let me begin with an observation about couples who are already married. Scripture tells husbands what to do, and Scripture tells wives what to do. The emphasis of the directives to husbands is that they should love their wives, as Christ loved the church (Eph. 5:25). The emphasis of the directives to wives is that they should respect and honor their husbands, submitting to them (Eph. 5:33). We have touched on this before, but here I would like to point out that these respective commands are not contingent upon the other person doing their bit. Husbands are not told to love their wives if their wives are being lovely. Or if their wives are being respectful. There is no *if* in it.

And by the same token, it does not say that wives are to be respectful to their husbands if their husbands are being respectable. Or if their husbands are being loving. There is no *if* in it. Now all of this assumes a marriage that simply an ordinary marriage between regular folks—we are not talking about radical forms of covenant-breaking. That's a different matter, which Scripture addresses in other places. So we are thinking of Joe and Jane Ordinary Christian, living down at the end of Ho Hum Lane. Love her, respect him.

So husbands are told to love, and wives are told to honor and respect. If you are already married, these are your marching orders, and you don't get to sit sullenly on the couch until the other one goes first. But here is the thing. When you are married, you don't get to think in terms of contingencies. But while you are still unattached, while you are being courted, you *do* get to think in terms of contingencies. You are wanting to determine if your assigned scriptural duties, if directed toward *this* man, would be a delight, or tedious, or a chore, or next to impossible.

In other words, in a marriage between sinners, fulfilling our duties toward one another will have its challenging moments, no matter who you are. But with that said, if you were to marry different men, this task of fulfilling your duty would be relatively difficult or *relatively* easy. You have the option now of seeing to it that it is relatively easy—because once you are married, that option is out. Once you are married, Scripture simply tells you to honor your husband, regardless of who he is. As long as you are in the plane, you can check your parachute as many times as you like. But once you have jumped, there you are.

As you are considering Trent, you should be asking yourself how readily (or not) he commands your respect. The central thing you should be looking for is your desire to respect him, honor him, follow him. You will be the blessing and glory of some man. Do you want *him* to get that glory? How challenging will it be for you if he gets that glory?

So with all this said, let me summarize three basic reasons why you must go into marriage prepared to honor, primed to respect.

The first is that Scripture flatly requires it. The Bible teaches us that wives are to be *obedient* to their husbands (Tit. 2:4-5). "Love, honor, and obey" will be in your wedding vows for a reason. Peter instructs wives *to be in subjection* to their own husbands (1 Pet. 3:1,5-6). Wives are to be subject to their husbands *in everything* (Eph. 5:22-25; Col. 3:18). As God is the head of Christ, and as Christ is the head of man, so also the man is the head of the woman (1 Cor. 11:3). This is not a teaching that is tucked away in some obscure corner of God's Word; it is pervasive. And then Peter tells women that they should be like the holy women of old, like Sara, calling her husband *lord* (1 Pet. 3:6).

What modern evangelicals have done is that they have rummaged around for an exegetical diluting agent, and having found one, they have poured it into all these texts, and so it is that the men have had *rule* taken away, and are charged to be *leaders* and, moreover, they must be *servant leaders*. Now I am not objecting to the servant part of this because Jesus did in actual fact lay down His life for His bride. That is what true masculinity is—the glad assumption of sacrificial responsibility. The sacrificial part of this is not the diluting agent. That part of it is biblical. But why leader and not lord? The Lord washed his disciples' feet, and He modeled for them how to be servant of all (Mark 10:44). But it was the *Lord* who did this: "If I then, your Lord and Master, have washed your feet; ye also ought to wash one another's feet" (John 13:14).

But no one talks about servant lordship the way they want to talk about servant leadership. The diluting agent move works better on "leaders." What this means is that you must come to understand that the levels of respect that God will expect you to render to Trent, assuming marriage, will be high. Lean into that responsibility, and if you think that this will be too much of a challenge for you, then say *no* now.

But before you say no, do a self-inventory. Ask yourself whether your hesitancy is because Trent is not "man enough" or because you have a feminist bone somewhere in your leg. That would mean Trent is not the problem, but rather you are. You are not yet "woman enough." So the kind of respect that God calls you to is not a mild sort of admiration.

The second reason is that this demeanor of obedience is an erotic necessity. There is a wonderful passage in *That Hideous Strength* where Ransom is explaining to Jane one of the reasons for her marital unhappiness. It is not the only reason, but it was one of the central ones. He says that she had lost love "because [she had] never attempted obedience."[1] When the scriptural structure of marital hierarchy is rejected, all sorts of dislocations result. And I write this knowing that my use of the word *hierarchy* here was a calloused use of a proscribed cringe word. In fact, all these words—obey, subjection, head, respect—are words that we moderns think unsuitable for this day and age. We, a

1. C.S. Lewis, *That Hideous Strength*, 145.

generation most miserable in our marriages, think we know better than the apostles of Jesus. But when we suppress this creational order, we are arguing with gravity . . . and that gravity will have its revenge. Not content with a biblically-ordered structure of authority and submission in marriage, we think that we can flatten the relationship between the sexes. The result is an eruption of demented caricatures of authority and submission—pagan things like *bondage* and submission, and other 50 shades of nonsense. We have rejected the kind of true authority that Jesus modeled and requires, because it might lead to abuses, and then turn around and celebrate fur-lined handcuffs, available at Amazon. So wisdom is justified by her children (Matt. 11:16-19).

And last, when you are living this way, you are doing so as a woman who fears the Lord—and a woman who fears the Lord is to be praised (Prov. 31:30). One of the consequences of being this kind of woman is that it builds trust: "Who can find a virtuous woman? For her price is far above rubies. *The heart of her husband doth safely trust in her*, so that he shall have no need of spoil" (Prov. 31:10–11, emphasis added).

Note that her husband trusts in her. Second, he safely trusts in her—she does not let him down. And third, the *heart* of her husband trusts in her. Do you want your marriage to be characterized by a fierce and dedicated loyalty? Do you want your husband to know that you are, to put it simply, doggedly *reliable*? Then this is the way.

Your uncle,
Douglas

SEVENTEEN

COURTSHIP AND SEXUAL BAGGAGE

Dear Darla,

So it is very good that your father is putting Trent through his paces. I take it that apart from the central question of your last letter, everything appears to be going swimmingly? So let's get to it. As to that central question, you raised the issue of his past porn use generally and, as it happens, your dad filled me in a little bit more on the phone last night. Your question is, "Does porn use in the past disqualify a suitor?" That was your father's question also—and the answer is, "No, it doesn't." At the same time, another answer would have to be, "Sometimes it can."

There are two issues involved in this. One is the question of repentance, forgiveness, and sanctification in the Christian life. The second has to do with whether the past behavior is any indication of likely future behavior. A woman has every right to stay far away from the kind of man whose enslavement to porn would be dragged into the marriage. Nobody needs that.

How you settle this will come down to what kind of man you believe Trent is. Most young Christian men believe that the Christian life consists of getting victory over sexual temptations. For many of them, that is the only temptation they are even really aware of. When they get married, and are given the great gift of sexual intimacy with their wife, they are greatly helped. It is not like temptation goes away entirely, but for most men, everything gets a lot more manageable. And this is precisely what Paul teaches. Marriage can be a great aid when it comes to godly continence (1 Cor. 7:9). But this is not the case for all men. Some men (5 percent, say) have deeper character issues that show up in the sexual realm—like contempt for women, or radical laziness, or hyper-competitiveness—and this shows up in bondage to porn, even though he has an active sex life with his wife.

The forgiveness issue has to do with sins in the past committed by the kind of guy who is in the 95 percent. Trust has to do with determining whether or not your suitor is in that 5 percent. Fortunately, most of the red flags that would indicate that problem can be seen outside the question of sexual history. Contempt for women, laziness, and hyper-competitiveness are all generally visible.

So let's deal with the forgiveness issue first, and then move on to the deal breaker aspect of it. All of us are sinners, and we all sin in various ways. As it happens, we live in pornified times, and the temptations for young men are ubiquitous. It used to be the case that to get your hands on porn you had to be seriously dedicated to that pursuit, and that included a willingness to head over to the seedy side of town. Now virtually every teen owns a portal to vast porn libraries, a portal they can carry around in their pocket or purse. I say "purse" because this is an increasing problem with young women, which is certainly not how it used to be. Almost always, the young men who get trapped by it are driven by lust, pure and simple. When women get trapped by it (not nearly as many as the men, but some), the issues are lust, insecurity about what they are supposed to be like, or curiosity about the competition. But it is a snare either way.

This being the case, it is not surprising that few young people today grow up without having had some scrape or other with pornography. And that is the situation Trent is in. From what your father tells me, he was snared by it when he was thirteen, had a couple of bad years, busted himself to his parents, and his father has helped him stay clean since, which has been about seven years give or take. So with those facts on the table before us, the question as to whether or not he should be disqualified as a potential husband should answer itself. Of course he should not be.

This is because he has an established pattern of victory over this temptation, and he has that pattern despite not having had any lawful sexual outlet. So when the question arises whether he could be a faithful husband, staying free of porn while married, once he does have a lawful sexual outlet, the answer would be, "Of course."

The only reason for saying no to him, in my view, would be the result of having an overly fastidious view of past sexual sins. Does Christ forgive us, or not? So this should not be a dealbreaker, not at all. You don't want to be in the position of a bank only willing to give a loan to customers who can prove that they don't need a loan.

But, as I am sure you know, forgiveness and trust are not the same thing. If another young man were showing interest in you, and your dad asked *him* about his prior porn use, and he replied that he "used to" have a problem "in the past," and your father then asked him how far in the past it was, and the answer was, "Up until about three weeks ago," the situation is different. But it would *not* be different on the forgiveness front. Christ can and does forgive the sins of three weeks ago as readily and as willingly as He forgives the sins of seven years ago. So forgiveness is not the issue. The issue would be trust. You do not yet know from this whether or not that young man has learned the lessons he needs to have learned in order to be a faithful husband. Forgiveness and trust are not the same thing at all—and lack of trust does not mean that there is a lack of forgiveness.

Because Trent has proven himself trustworthy on this issue, over the course of *years*, it is the most sensible thing in the world to trust him. So if his past use of porn remained an issue to you, that would mean that you were struggling with an unbiblical view of forgiveness. Christ has cleansed him, and yet you are regarding him as not yet fully cleansed.

The fact that it would be an unbiblical view of forgiveness can be readily illustrated with a thought experiment. Suppose a young man came around, showing interest in one of your close friends, one of your roommates. They began to date, and everyone who knew them thought they were *perfect* for each other.

After a time, the relationship grew serious enough that they had to have "the talk," the one in which sexual histories were discussed. Now suppose that your friend had lost her virginity during high school, during a short stretch when she was backslidden, and in rebellion against her parents (who were godly Christian folks). She was a professing, baptized Christian during this time, but not at all serious about her faith. Then there was a crisis during her senior year which God used to wake her up spiritually, and she repented, fully and completely. She believes that she was actually converted, regenerated, at that time. And all that was seven years ago, say. But however forgiven she is now, she is still not a virgin. Forgiveness removes the sting of the law, but does not alter natural consequences. If she had gotten pregnant, however forgiven she was, she would still be a mother in the present. The kid wouldn't disappear.

But although your friend didn't get pregnant, she did sleep with her boyfriend a handful of times, and that is now seven years in the past, long repented. Now suppose her current boyfriend really stumbles over this information. Suppose it has always been very important to him that he marry a virgin, and so this news throws him for a loop. He has not made any decision yet, but he is struggling mightily with it. Now this is just a thought experiment, but let me rush to the happy ending so that nobody gets too upset with this hypothetical guy. They *do* get together and live happily ever after. Don't be angry at him any more.

But while he is making up his mind, what is the attitude of all the girls in your apartment toward him? What do all the roomies think of him? "Jerk. Pig. A la-di-dah suitor. She's way too good for him anyhow. Pharisee." But the thing he is dealing with is the exact same question we are dealing with regarding Trent. And we don't think *we* are being jerks simply because we want to take this information into account. It *should* be factored in.

Our culture makes it easy to weigh such things with unequal weights and measures on sexual matters because we live in a time when women must be forgiven all manner of wrongs or can do no wrong, and men are considered guilty of all things sexual by definition. And so then, when the men actually *have* been guilty of a sexual trespass, it is easy to just hang the spirit of the age around their necks. Everybody would think this guy was being harsh with your roommate, but nobody would think that you are being harsh with Trent.

So with all of that said, on the basis of what you wrote, and what your father told me, I don't think that this information should even slow you down. I pray that it hasn't slowed him down. If you think it has, just wink at him.

Your uncle,
Douglas

EIGHTEEN

A DIFFERENT KIND OF DADDY ISSUE

Dear Darla,

So I take it that things are getting a mite serious over there. Good for you. I trust you are smiling at him brightly?

That apparently being the case, let me compare and contrast two different kinds of daddy issues. When a father has been a good father to his daughter, as yours obviously has been, despite being a great blessing, it nevertheless creates a unique set of challenges. When a father has been distant, or abdicating, or abusive, this creates another set of

challenges—what are popularly known as "daddy issues." As your dad has been a strong father,
both to you and your siblings, this does not remove
the possibility of something going wrong—it just
changes the nature of what could go wrong.

So let me begin with the situation that you are
likely to encounter, and then I will compare it to the
other kind of situation, the really sad kind.

A father has an entirely different relationship to
his daughters than he does with his sons. It is not
the case that he just has generic "kids," and provided he treats them well, everything will unfold
in exactly the same way. No. He is a man, and he
is a man with sons and daughters. A good father is
modeling for his sons what *they* should want to be
like, while he is doing something very different for
his daughters. For them he is modeling what they
should want a future husband to be like. A similar
thing happens on the other side, with mothers and
daughters and mothers and sons. In this case, he is
modeling the kind of man you should *want*, not the
kind of man you should *be*.

The paradigm for all of this was established in
the Garden of Eden, long ago: "Therefore shall a
man leave his father and his mother, and shall
cleave unto his wife: and they shall be one flesh"
(Genesis 2:24; cf. Matt. 19:5).

Sons leave. Daughters are given. This means a son
"detaches" from his father in a manner that is very
different than how a daughter detaches—although

they both are separated from their families of origin in order to form a new family unit.

When the apostle Paul is writing about the different requirements for the sexes in the course of a service of worship, he says this: "Let your women keep silence in the churches: for it is not permitted unto them to speak; but they are commanded to be under obedience, *as also saith the law*" (1 Cor. 14:34).

As the law also says. But where does the law *say* that?

The most likely candidate is found in Numbers 30, the passage that talks about how to manage it when a daughter or a wife has made a vow to the Lord. I won't quote the passage at length here, but it is worth looking up and reading through carefully (Num. 30:3-16). In that passage if a woman vows something to the Lord, her father has the authority to abrogate that vow when he first hears of it. But if he hears of it and says nothing, then her vow stands. This shows how even an abdicating father is held responsible. His inaction is treated by the law of God as action. If this young woman then marries, the same principle carries over to her new husband. If he hears of it, and says nothing, then the vow stands.

This shows that there is an analogous relation between a father and daughter and a husband and a daughter. Both a father and a husband are *heads*, and at a wedding that covenantal headship is transferred: "But I would have you know, that the head of every man is Christ; and the head of the woman is the man; and the head of Christ is God" (1 Cor. 11:3).

If the head of the woman is the man, referring to her husband, if we place these passages together, this means that her father was her covenant head before she was married.

"And why are you bringing all this up?" you might be asking. "I'm in love, and so why the deep theology?"

Well, this is all going to be enormously practical in just a few months. The stronger and tighter your relationship with your dad, the more of a challenge it will be transferring that allegiance to a different man. Not only that, but a different man who is thirty years younger than your dad, and that much more inexperienced, and who doesn't have the same kind of deep account with you that your father does. About the only thing he has over your father is that he can probably run faster.

But it is not hopeless. What he has going for him is that this whole thing is apparently a design feature. God intends for this to be done, and so when it is done right, it really is glorious. But there are ways in which it can be done poorly, ineptly, or not at all. So it is a father's task to have his daughter's emotional bank account full, topped off. But he has to do this in such a way as enables her to transfer it all to another bank.

If he does this right, he is giving a new and inexperienced husband a head start, and time enough to learn the ropes. The new husband can draw on the account that the father established. But if dad is the wrong kind of alpha father, he is going to have trouble letting go, or his daughter might have trouble letting go, or both, and this is how the poor daughter becomes the rope in a tug-of-war. One of the temptations that comes to strong fathers is the temptation of viewing strong sons-in-law as *competition* somehow. This is the set up for all kinds of problems.

When your dad gives you away, he is such a gracious Christian gentleman, I have no doubt that he will do it right. But sometimes daughters don't have their father's wisdom, and they compare their husbands to their dads in the wrong way. And there are fathers, and I am afraid that I have seen them, who give their daughter's hand ceremonially during the wedding, but in no other way. They don't really let go, in other words.

A young couple needs to fix it in their minds that they are establishing a new covenant household, that as households go, has the same rank as the households they grew up in. The household of "the kids" is not an annex to or extension of the households of the groom's family, or of the bride's. After the wedding, we have three households, not two-and-a-half. You don't want your oldest child to be sixteen when he experiences his first Thanksgiving in his own house.

I know your folks very well, and I know that they are committed to this principle that I am describing, and so I know they are not going to be difficult.

But this should be one of your expectations for Trent. You should be considering whether or not he is the kind of man who will shield you from your well-meaning in-laws, or if your folks were being difficult, from them as well. If you were getting undue pressure from his mother, or from your father (which we obviously do not expect), he is the kind of man who will step in between. Will he be the kind of man who would say, "Mom, we really want to hear your concerns, and we will consider them, and pray through them. But you really need to bring them to me, and not to Darla." Good fences make good neighbors—and a good man is a good fence.

Compare all this to the other kind of problem. If a young woman has the other kind of daddy issues, she can't get away from home fast enough. Or at least it appears that way. But she has a vacuum inside, and she is looking for a way to fill it up. It is a vacuum that is shaped like an authoritative male head, and so she takes her father-void, her father hunger, with her. This is why she so easily latches on or clings to a man, or to men, to anyone that she thinks might be able to fill that void. And so she goes off to empower herself through pole dancing, or some other way of disappointing her father. Of course, there is no shortage of men around, but none of these men can fill that void, and a good two-thirds of them don't even want to. They just pretend to want to in order to get her into bed, and then they are gone like the whistling wind. And just like the whistling wind, they never call anymore.

But in a healthy situation, as I said above, the father of the bride is giving the new husband a head start. He is beginning a new venture in the establishment of this household, and a godly father has been the financier, a venture capitalist. When a secure daughter transfers her allegiance to her new head (which is not the same thing as transferring loyalty, affection, or respect), she is doing something that should come naturally. She loves and respects her dad, as always, but her allegiance has been transferred. She is a naturalized citizen of another country now. A woman used to carry her father's name, and now her last name is the name of her husband.

When feminists kick at this, thinking they are subverting the patriarchy, they are not actually keeping their womanly name. They are doggedly sticking with their father's name, and their grandfather's, and their great-grandfather's. They are being narrowly patriarchal in this. A Christian maiden is brought up knowing that a woman is not bound to one male line forever. She knows that each generation of daughters is privileged to bring new life to a new line.

This is God's design. A woman is supposed to take her husband's name. This is not a quaint Anglo-Saxon custom; it is fully biblical: "Male and female created he them; and blessed them, and called their name Adam, in the day when they were created" (Gen. 5:2).

God created us male and female, and placed his blessing upon *that*, and called *their* name Mr. and Mrs. Adam. All the LGBTQ+ business is nothing less than hostility toward the blessings of God. You should therefore relinquish your father's name, and you should do it with joy. When your dad gives you away, it is so that you might take a name other than his, and that should bring him great joy. How could it not? It is God's design.

> With gladness and rejoicing they shall be brought; They shall enter the King's palace. *Instead of Your fathers shall be Your sons*, whom You shall make princes in all the earth. (Ps. 45:15–16, emphasis added)

Your uncle,
Douglas

NINETEEN

WEDDING AS ADORNMENT

Dear Darla,

I hear from Nancy via your mother that Trent has proposed, and that you have accepted. So good job, everybody. Now we're talking.

If you will permit me just one more short letter, allow me to tie this happy thing off with just a few surrounding observations. In all the happiness and excitement of getting ready for marriage, and with all the planning for the wedding, it is sometimes easy to forget which is the gift and which is the al-tar. Here is what I mean.

Let me begin by defining what it is that consti-tutes a marriage. What is it that causes a marriage to come into existence? There are two elements, and neither one is necessarily what we would call ceremonial. Those two elements are, first, the covenant that is struck, in a manner recognized by the society in which the marriage is happening, and the second element is the sexual consummation. When both these conditions have been met, then you have a marriage, and if only one of them has, then you do not yet have a marriage. If covenant vows are taken, but there is no consummation, then it is not a marriage. If sex has occurred, but no covenant, then there is no marriage.

So first a note about what it means to be societally recognized. It is not just a matter of promising—it has to be a covenant promise, and it needs to be publicly binding. If a young man gets his girlfriend into the back seat of a car by promising to love her "forever and a day," that is not a covenant. He is trying to get *around* his social obligations and is not contracting social obligations. He is making and breaking a personal promise, but it does not have the force of a covenant. In different societies there might be different performative rites that mean the covenant is made—exchanging rings is what we usually do—but the thing that matters is that the covenant commitment is made and everybody knows about it.

Now if a couple get married by a justice of the peace, and the "ceremony" is conducted over a formica counter top at the county courthouse, it is a

ceremony with no frills, right? But the society recognizes it, and a couple married in that way have
the same obligations before the law as a couple who
got married in a cathedral, with the bride entering
on the back of an elephant to Ravel's *Bolero*. The
ceremonial aspects do not create the covenantal
obligations, but rather (when done right) simply respect and honor and adorn those obligations. And
this kind of honor is commanded in Scripture: "Let
marriage be held in honor among all, and let the
marriage bed be undefiled, for God will judge the
sexually immoral and adulterous" (Heb. 13:4).

When we have a nice church wedding, and we
all gather for it, we are *honoring* marriage. We are
making a big deal out of it. But as the honor becomes more and more ornate, it creates at least the
temptation for us to forget what it is we are actually
doing. This is what is happening (in extreme forms)
when the wedding prep makes absolutely everyone
miserable because the bride has become bridezil-
la. Instead of the wedding adorning the marriage,
the wedding has taken on a life of its own, and it is
kind of a ceremonial mutant. This is what I meant
by comparing it to the Lord's jab about the gold and
the temple, or the gift and the altar. Everything is
twisted backwards.

It is the marriage that makes the wedding important, not the wedding that makes the marriage important. The exchange of covenant vows
starts the process of forming the marriage, which

will be completed later that evening at the hotel. This means that the wedding is the doorway into the marriage. The various ceremonies we have are decorations of that door—like a Christmas wreath on your door during Advent. They do not create or frame the door, but rather simply adorn it.

The old hymn "The Sands of Time are Sinking," refers to this truth:

> The bride eyes not her garment,
> But her dear Bridegroom's face;
> I will not gaze at glory
> But on my King of grace.

Your task is to focus on Trent, and do not in any way sacrifice your relationship to him, or to anyone else either, for the sake of the decorated doorway. You want the ceremony to be a true adornment of your marriage, and not some third thing that enters into some kind of weird competition with your marriage.

And this brings us to the second element that constitutes a marriage, which is the sexual consummation. In my experience talking about this, this is something that a good many tender-hearted Christians struggle with. They think it is endearing and sweet when a quadriplegic "marries" his high school sweetheart, regardless of the accident that rendered him incapable of consummating the marriage. To be clear, I have no objection to such arrangements—I just don't want to call it a marriage. Marriage is a one-flesh union, sealed with a covenant. That is what it *is*.

This is why the category of annulment is needed, as something distinct from divorce. Say a couple get married, and for whatever reason the union is not consummated. Say that the bride has an emotional melt down and refuses. Or say that the groom is unable to perform. A couple in such straits should seek out marital counseling immediately, and they should work through their issues until their union is successfully consummated. Great, happy ending. But if it is not resolved, their marital union should be annulled, not dissolved. It is not *there* to be dissolved. The scriptural criteria for lawful divorce don't apply. It is not the same thing.

It is good for you and your mother to adorn the marriage with a ceremony that honors this reality, but we must never forget that the sexual act is just about the most unceremonious thing in the world. And so, sometimes young Christian women are distracted by the ceremonial honor, and then can be somewhat startled when the whole thing turns overtly sexual.

But this is what marriage *is*. It is a covenant that surrounds and binds a sexual relationship. Now I am not saying that marriages are kept together by sex and sex alone. No, of course not. Hollywood is crammed full of sexy people who can't for the life of them stay married to each other. Compare all of this to a meal. Scripture tells us that it is better to have thin carrot soup with harmony than to have feasting with strife (Prov. 17:1). But we should at least be able to agree that there needs to be food of some sort on the table. That is what a meal *is*.

We look forward to getting your invitation. It will be great seeing you all again, and I look forward to meeting Trent.

Your uncle,
Douglas

Made in the USA
Middletown, DE
11 June 2024

55444569R00097